bullycide
IN AMERICA

MOMS SPEAK OUT

ABOUT THE BULLYING/SUICIDE CONNECTION

Cover Illustration: Brandon Johnson
Graphics Director and Editing: JBS Publishing, Inc – Darlington MD.

This book is available by print on demand, on Amazon.com

bullycide
IN AMERICA

MOMS SPEAK OUT

ABOUT THE
BULLYING/SUICIDE
CONNECTION

Compiled by Brenda High

Contributors include:
Brenda High, Michelle Calco, Tammy Epling, Summer Himes,
Debra Johnston, Cathy Swartwood Mitchell and Rochelle Sides

Special Submissions by
Judy Kuczynski, Adrianna Sgarlata Schweizer,
Robin Todd and The Readings

Special Thanks:
Writer, Author, Publisher – Fern Smith Brown

Contents

Special submissions

Appendices

Dedications

Dedicated to Jeffrey Scott Johnston who will always be my Golden Child; to Nicole Guntrip for carrying me through the nights when I could not stand, to Jeb Bush and Ellyn Bogdanoff for giving Jeff a voice; to family, friends, schools, and the people of Lee County; and finally to all the members and associates of Students for Safer Schools. "We are family!"

Debra Johnston

I dedicate this book to my husband Kevin (my best friend) to Kristen, my daughter (my ray of sunshine) to family and dear friends. May we all continue to be courageous and honest as we travel through our grief. And to my son, Matt (my precious gift) whose love I will carry forever in my heart.

Tammy Epling

To my husband Johnny, if I had one friend left, I'd want it to be you, I love you. To my sons Michael, Ronald and Richard, it's an honor to be your mother. To Hillary, you made it possible to feel joy again, I love you baby. To my sisters, we will forever be the Jackson 5. Jewel, thank you for loving me unconditionally, you are the mother I always hoped to be.

Rochelle Sides

To my dear, dear family, God Bless them, every one.

Michelle Calco

To my son Daniel, who has given unconditional love, support and words of wisdom— beyond his years. To my Mom and Dad for always being. To Randy, for being a wonderful father to our two boys. To Todd, who came into my life at one of my lowest points and who loves me. To friends and strangers who have given endless support....To God, who listened.

Cathy Swartwood Mitchell

To my husband, Bill, and my children Sonja, Jacob and Tara. It's been a long road of healing but we have stood strong together.

Brenda High

Dedicated to my angel April, who I hold close to my heart, every minute of every day. Thank you, my children, Marlena, Scotty and Gregg. To my grandchildren Willow, Scarlett and Mason. To Rob and Annie Norris for letting April become a member of their family. To my best friends, Jimmy Walke and Judy Gowey, for teaching me what service really means.

Summer Himes

BULLYCIDE AWARENESS DAY

WHEREAS, on April 20th, 1999, our Nation's worst high school shooting in Littleton, Colorado, took place at Columbine High School; the terror ended in the death of many students and a teacher along with several students who were wounded; *Columbine was real*; and

WHEREAS, on September 11, 2001, terrorists attacked the United States; in New York City, some 3000 men and women, including firefighters, police officers and paramedics were killed, leaving an unforgettable mark in U.S. history and in our hearts and memories; *9/11 was real*; and

WHEREAS, educators, parents and community members recognize the lessons to be taken from these tragedies and be proactive in preventing the beginning of such destructive behavior that is in our schools today; bullying...*school terrorism...is real*; and

WHEREAS, many children are faced with terror, daily, through harassment, assaults and verbal threats in our schools, on the playground, on school busses; for many children school is a battlefield; thus, a source of terrorism; and

WHEREAS, educators must come together with parents and community members to safeguard schools for our children, and, through our recognition of the serious issues that face them each day, offer our children a school environment that provides a positive, safe and secure learning climate – where all children feel they belong, and know that they are respected for who they are - promoting excellence in citizenship; and one that includes a bully prevention program to help ensure fair and effective discipline; and

WHEREAS, educators, parents and community members have publicly expressed concern about the war in our schools – the bullying of our children; it is important that we acknowledge and heighten awareness about this serious issue, and the negative effects of bullying, including the long-term damage it can cause; far too often bullying results in "bullycide" a suicide attributed to bullying; and

WHEREAS, it is the personal responsibility of all citizens to protect our children; it is time for us to stand up, speak out and take action against bullying; and

WHEREAS, in remembrance of 9/11 and Columbine High School, and the loved ones that have been lost to the tragic effects of bullying, and bullycide, we must persevere in our year-round battle against bullying, and it is appropriate that we designate September 29th or the last Tuesday in September each year, as Bullycide Awareness Day.

Written by Robin Todd, Bully Police Arizona Director

Acknowledgements

I want to thank some special people who made this book and its contents possible.

To Bully Police USA Consultant, Catherine Hogan, for encouraging me to develop my ideas into reality. Thank you Robin Todd, Bully Police Arizona Director, for helping me put together the content for this book.

To Shelley Norman for helping with the initial editing, a painful experience because of a recent loss of a child, your continued support helped me to stay the course. To Chris and Eric Reading for editing the entire book...not an easy job when working with 10 (women) writers!

To the Friends and Volunteers of Bully Police USA - Your painful stories inspired me to get the book finished as quickly as possible.

Thank you to the many lawmakers who have worked to get anti bullying laws passed in their state. I would especially like to thank Representatives Tom Trail and Pete Nielsen of Idaho who pushed and passed "Jared's Law", the anti bullying law in Idaho (2006). That meant so much to me.

To the writers and mothers who put up with my constant "reminder" calls, emails and conference calls, always pushing. You put up with a lot, but your patience has been wonderful. I have been inspired by each of you and I thank you. We became a sisterhood because of our painful experiences. I know that we will make a difference for many other moms who will read our stories and then speak out as well.

All my life I have been blessed with wonderful family and friends. Thank you. You have helped to uplift and support me when I needed it most.

To my husband, Bill, who put up with my long hours and late night vigils during the writing of this book. Without your love and patience, this book would not have been possible. To my daughter Sonja, and son-in-law Larry, thank you for your support; thank you for giving Bill and I two sweet grandsons, Jared and David. It was a great honor to your little brother's memory when you named your son, Jared, after Jared Benjamin High. To Jacob and my daughter-in-law Suzanne, who loves Jacob - you are both a great joy in my life. Finally, to my youngest daughter, Tara, who was the baby that rarely cried and always wanted to be cuddled, you are the sweetness in my life.

Brenda L. High

3

Foreword

By Judy M. Kuczynski MS

This is not a book about blame or guilt, although it may certainly spark that kind of discussion. This is not a book about getting even or setting the record straight, although it may do that as well. And, this is not a book for clinicians, although it will offer some scientific data and educational resources.

This is a book of real stories about real kids. Kids who took their own lives because they thought it was their only way out of a hopeless situation. It is about the tragic choices they made in an effort to end the pain - when they believed there was no other solution.

It is told by mothers who are willing to share their own personal pain as they watched their children suffer and struggle. It is about their own efforts to advocate for their children while they continue to deal with their own devastating loss and the aftermath of bullycide.

The culture of harassment and bullying among today's youth has no socio-economic bounds. It is problem that has grown to epidemic proportions and is prevalent in all strata of our society. These kids could be your kids.

This is a book about bullycide – the act taken by the victim of bullying to end his or her life.

There is much debate about the role of bullying in teen suicide. However, we do know that teen suicide has tripled over the past 50 years. The National Youth Violence Prevention Resource Center [NYVPRC] reports that suicide is the third leading cause of death among teenagers - almost 2,000 teens are successful in their attempts to end their lives each year. It is important to note that this is the number of attempts that actually succeed. The National Institute of Mental Health estimates that only one-in-six (some experts report that only one-in-ten) suicide attempts are successful!

We know that bullying has recently been recognized as a common behavior among adolescents. The Center for Disease Control reports that over 5.7 million teens in the United States, or more than 30% are estimated to be involved in bullying as bully, victim, or both. Even the CDC admits that accurate data is limited - making it more likely that these numbers are low estimates.

Researchers acknowledge that within the teen population, there is a "high prevalence of bullying behaviors." And, within that same group of teens, they also see risky and unsafe behaviors, although they have been reluctant to build a simple case of cause and effect. In an article about school bullying by *Family First Aid: Help for troubled teens*, the author reports that in desperation teens may carry weapons for protection or revenge or "even consider suicide."

The mothers who tell their stories in this book do not need researchers or experts to make the connection between bullying and suicide. They know firsthand that as long as we intellectualize this phenomenon and debate it, it will remain an impersonal subject of speculation, avoidance, paralysis, guilt, and blame rather than one of responsibility and change.

This book is for those of you with young children, who will soon be preteens and teenagers. It is for those with teenagers. It is for grandparents who are watching over loved ones. This book is for people who work in law enforcement, health care, education, or in any profession involving children and teenagers. It is for concerned citizens who simply want to be educated so they can help to make a difference.

I invite you all into the reality of these stories, and the struggle revealed by these mothers to transform the pain and senseless loss of a beloved child into something that gives hope and life to all young people, and their families.

Introduction

Bullycide...A Lesson and a Warning!
A parent's perspective... by Brenda High (Jared's mom)

The Mission
Bullycide in America is designed as a tool to raise awareness, inform and educate all people that bullying and its tragic consequences are a real phenomenon. And through this education we will enact change for future prevention.

Bullycide
What is Bullycide? In this book we will examine many stories of bullycide, all a little bit different, yet all connected. What was it that caused these wonderful children to take such drastic measures? Were there consistent elements that played a role in these tragic events?

It is common knowledge among mental health specialists and those knowledgeable on the subject of depression that more than 90 percent of people who die by suicide have depression or another diagnosable mental or substance abuse disorder, (www.SpanUSA.org), among adults, among teenagers. The question, therefore, must be asked, what causes depression?

A person just doesn't wake up one morning with depression. Psychologists believe that some people have a genetic tendency towards depression, some people develop depression because of environmental triggers, and some people can have both genetic and environmental triggers. Perhaps our children were more sensitive than most. And therefore, were more susceptible to the effects of the torment they endured.

However, every parent in this book firmly believes that the environmental factors affecting our children were the root cause of their depression, and ultimate suicide. Every story in this book is about depression, and the bullying that triggered it. The new term being used to describe this type of depression-caused teen suicide is, "bullycide."

The Lesson
Sometimes it is only through the hard lessons of others that we learn what path we should take in our lives...but it doesn't usually start out that way.

We watch our parents when we are young. We learn values, and begin to develop a sense of who we are. We watch our friends, we make mistakes, and we grow. We learn in school, from our teachers, not just math and science, reading and writing, but life lessons. Hopefully, we develop a sense of social conscience and how we can, in some way, contribute to the greater good. Sometimes...we have no idea where the lesson will come from. What singular event, good or bad, might change our entire lives, and point us to that life-path. We, the parents of children who chose to die by suicide, find ourselves in this place...on a new and unexpected path. We want others to understand how we have come to be here, and the avoidable tragedies that brought us to the depths of despair, the same tragedies that have set us on a new path...of action. These unbearable events have shaped our current lives and set us on a course, to share our lessons and offer our insights through our stories. We pray others may learn from us.

Our stories, six others, and mine, are deeply personal and tragic. We have all had a very hard time writing those stories; it is difficult to express the emotion that comes from losing a child by suicide, or by bullycide, as we now call it. At the time of this writing, some in our group lost their children years ago, others, much more recently. Still, as difficult as it was to share these events, in many ways it was healing. We were (and are) able to honor our children, their lives, their souls; they were fantastic people who deserve to be remembered. By remembering them in this fashion, and sharing what we have learned, we hope we can truly make a difference in the lives of others.

What are some of the lessons have we learned?
One thing I know we have learned, along with the ins and outs of bullying in today's world, is a different respect for the power of bullying. Collectively, our knowledge and experience on the subject rivals any clinical or educational endeavor. I won't say what the other moms have experienced, but for me, I have lived the subject of bullying, spoke about bullying and enacted change regarding bullying since the day my son Jared died. Many have called me a "Mom on a Mission", to stop school bullying. That calling is in my heart, and will be for many, many years.

I know the mothers in this book have learned about the soul of a victim, in this case, their own child. Our children suffered (mostly) quietly, until one day, these gentle-soul individuals took their pain out on themselves in one explosive, self-destructive act. They were captive to the thoughts inside their sensitive minds. Strongly influenced by the events and kids around them, and beaten down by chronic bullying, they were convinced that to live was not worth fighting for, and to die was their only escape.

As parents, we have learned that it is difficult to be a "survivor". It isn't so much as being left alone on an island; the real torture comes from being left alone in one's mind...to deal with one's thoughts, but being forced to live with mind-demons day by day.

The Warning

When you look at the pictures of our children, you cannot help but notice that they were normal children, with normal faces. They had normal personalities with normal feelings and emotions. They were just kids in every way.

You have undoubtedly heard it said, in many contexts, "If it could happen to me, it could happen to you". This is as true as true can be. No one is immune. No child, no family, no community. Bullying exists everywhere, in many forms; and its tragic consequences are very real.

To offer insight, the moms have assembled some of our own personal messages in the form of short warnings:

- **Rochelle Sides** – "Don't be afraid of the school, the teachers or administrators. You must remember they work for you, and your children. If you don't stand up for your child, who will?"
- **Debra Johnston** – "A bully doesn't have to be eye to eye to bully someone. Sometimes he or she gets into cyberspace, and then there's no place to hide from their torment."
- **Summer Himes** – "Bullies WILL cause depression and depression is the number one cause of suicide. The signs are there – be aware!"
- **Brenda High** – "It's your child. You must fight for him or her. No one cares like a parent cares - a parent is motivated by love."
- **Michelle Calco** – "If you *think* something is wrong, something is probably wrong. Go with your gut feelings."
- **Tammy Epling** – "Don't be fooled. Bullying doesn't have to be repeated, or take place over a period of time. Each child is different. Even one traumatic instance can cripple a young mind into a well of despair."
- **Cathy Swartwood Mitchell** – "While you are going through the system to fight for your child's rights, your child is the one going into the battlefield...and today could be the day that he or she is fatally wounded."

We all deal with grief and despair differently, but only those who have lost a loved one to suicide can understand the gamut of emotions that come with losing a loved one by this means – it just isn't the same. It's hard to tell people I meet, who ask me how my youngest child died, that he died by suicide/bullycide. It would be so much easier to say, "Jared died in a tragic accident." But the truth cannot be hidden, and as the scripture says, "The truth shall make you free."

Although this book is filled with sad stories, it is a book about hope. It is our desire to help others, and educate those who read our stories, so that they do not have to endure the same sad fate someday. In talking to the other parents who have contributed their stories to this book, I have found we've all learned common lessons, among them, patience, endurance, empathy and understanding. Our crying eyes have dried, a little, and our shaking hands have stilled, a bit.

We are now ready to share our stories.

"Like Thieves in the Night"

"While you are going through the system to fight for your child's rights, your child is the one going into the battlefield.... and today could be the day that he or she is fatally wounded."

Brandon's Story
Bullies Who Kill

In loving memory of
Brandon Chris Swartwood - 2/21/82 – 12/16/00
By Cathy Swartwood Mitchell

I wrote an email message to Brenda High four months after Brandon's death. It began as a commentary after I read about Charles "Andy" Williams and the shooting at Santana High School in California. Brenda responded, asking me if she could post it on her website at jaredstory.com. That was the beginning of a friendship and a sistership between Brenda and me. Only someone who has lost a child to bullying can begin to understand and relate to me now. With my permission, Brenda omitted some of the references to Andy Williams and the Santana School shooting. There have been many school shootings — although many more children die by bullycide. Perhaps I chose to write something when I read about the Santana shooting because I had just lost Brandon. Perhaps it was close to my heart because I lived in Santee, California (near Santana High School), as a child. The posting of "Brandon's Story" on Brenda's website was the beginning of my activism. Brenda has assisted others like me and has single-handedly done more to help the victims of bullying and those who have lost loved ones to bullycide than any other individual I know. Brenda is my mentor. I have now added a little more detail about what happened to Brandon, my beloved son. I pray that somehow this will contribute to understanding and awareness, and someday, this epidemic will end.

I have tried to write Brandon's story for three days and have not been able to complete it...maybe today. I have a lot to say and this is a very painful and emotional subject for me. While my heart goes out to the victims of all school shootings, a different type of crime is happening in our schools. It has devastated my life.

Although rarely labeled as such, "bullying" is a crime. It injures, maims, destroys and kills. Until a proactive approach is taken against crimes of bullying, a reactive approach to crimes of school shootings is futile. Bullying is a crime in which the perpetrators are rarely punished and the victims rarely receive justice. This crime is usually repetitive and a victim is injured and traumatized over and over again. When bullying claims yet another victim, few notice and even fewer care.

Oftentimes, the victims themselves are blamed by being told that they must be doing something to "deserve" it. These victims are isolated and usually suffer in silence. The media doesn't broadcast the injuries or deaths of these silenced victims. Our nation doesn't share in their pain or extend sympathies to their survivors. Communities aren't outraged by these senseless and equally devastating crimes. The only outrage in our nation — in our communities — is when the psychological injuries caused by the bullying are externalized, and we have yet another school shooting.

In the adult world, we have laws against bullying. We do not tolerate these crimes in our workplace. Yet, our children are told they must tolerate this in their workplace — our schools. Society, in general, has the mindset that it is "all right" or "a rite of passage" for bullies to deliberately and systematically destroy their victims — our children.

Why, but why, would anyone ask our impressionable children to endure more than we as adults do? How could anyone expect our children to make it through humiliation, torment, isolation, assaults or brutal beatings unscathed? We shouldn't. And they don't.

In the adult world, these crimes have names like harassment and battery. Yet society uses different terms when the victims are children. I must pose this question to law enforcement, school administrators and our society. At what age does teasing become harassment, taunting become tormenting, following become stalking, punching become assaulting, or a fight become a battery? As long as we ignore such questions, the ignorant mindset prevails, and our most vulnerable will continue to be our least protected.

Yes, some kids will survive being bullied just like some adults survive being victimized. However, in both instances the injuries and the recovery depend largely on the number, frequency, severity and duration of the crimes.

A great many will leave school to escape being victimized. They will be deprived of an education — a small price to pay to escape the torment and humiliation. Some children will leave their hometowns to get away from the harassment and torture. Some children will turn to substance abuse and self-medicate in an attempt to escape their pain and suffering. Some will lose all self-confidence and come to believe there must be something wrong with them — just like others said.

Some children will leave this world to escape their living hell on earth — since their pain is with them wherever they go.

Other children will learn to accept the physical and psychological injuries inflicted upon them "just for fun." They will go to doctors, take their medications, and accept the fact that life isn't fair. They won't question the system or ask why they were not allowed to get a public education, just because someone didn't like the way they dressed, or perhaps the way they looked. It could have been that they were really intelligent or perhaps that they really struggled to learn. Maybe the bullies accused them of being a Christian or a Satanist...gay or straight...rich or poor. You get the picture.

At any rate, these bullies set themselves up as judge, jury and executioner — depriving their victims of their education, their health and their happiness. Surely, we should expect the victims to be okay — to come through this uninjured and unscathed.

When we don't acknowledge bullying as a real crime, we dismiss the very real injuries inflicted upon the victims. Although the psychological injuries and extent can be varied, they are real injuries. Sometimes, the symptoms are internalized, and sometimes they are externalized. (Sometimes both) In either case, bullying kills and children die.

I speak from experience. My beloved son, Brandon, was a victim of bullies.

Brandon developed post traumatic stress disorder (PTSD) and depression after being harassed, tormented, isolated, assaulted and brutally beaten in our public school system. When we took out a protective order against one of the bullies, the boy sent a friend to the principal's office to claim that Brandon had made a bomb threat. Everything considered, the accusation was absurd — but the way the school handled the allegation was shameful.

After meeting with Brandon and me, an administrator called me saying, "I have some good news and some bad news. The good news is that I have been asking some kids if they think Brandon Swartwood is capable of bombing the school, and basically, they all said 'no.'" He continued with, "The bad news is that one kid said that he thought that Brandon was a little strange — but he didn't think he was a bomber." In short, the administrator finished with a statement that he thought might upset me — that another kid thought Brandon was a little strange.

My son had been accused of making a bomb threat and the school had poured fuel on the fire by spreading the rumor with their questioning. They thought that I would be upset about the "strange" comment from one other student? Appalled, I responded with, "You have been asking students if they think that Brandon is capable of bombing the school? Do you realize what you have done?" Within a few days, I received another call from the administrator, telling me that "this thing is out of control" and they needed me to come up to the school. He said they were receiving calls from parents asking what they had done with the Swartwood kid. He told me this "thing" was spreading "like wildfire." What did they expect, when the school administration had provided the fuel!

I arrived at the school and was seated in the administrator's office. Within minutes I heard a commotion. A coach came running into the front office saying, "Hasben" (name I'll assign to this bully), "just knocked the shit out of Brandon Swartwood — hit him in the back of the head in the hall." Brandon came into the office visibly upset with a huge red mark on the back of his neck. The coach went back out and got Hasben. Hasben came in yelling obscenities as the administrator tried to calm him down.

During our meeting, the administrator told me that he didn't think that Brandon had made the bomb threat, but that it was so out of control that they could not protect him. There were only five days left in Brandon's junior year. They said if we would take him home, they would give him his grades, as they stood, without taking the semester exams.

I told them we were in an impossible situation. "If I leave him in school, you are telling me that you can't protect him. If I agree to pull him out, others will believe the allegation, (of the bomb threat), was substantiated and Brandon has been expelled." Students had been yelling at Brandon in the halls, saying things like, "Am I on your hit list?" and "Die Swartwood." I had no choice but to pull him for the remainder of the year.

The damage Brandon sustained over this incident alone was beyond measure. The assistant principal later told me that he was "convinced" that Brandon had not made the bomb threat. Unfortunately, the damage to Brandon could not be undone. Brandon had to live with the stigma of the "would-be bomber."

This is just one of the incidents Brandon endured. There were many.

I tried to transfer Brandon to another school district that summer. The transfer was denied, so he went back to Coweta that fall. Within a few weeks, he was brutally beaten in the school cafeteria.

Brandon had surgery to repair his physical injuries. I notified the school of his surgery and the estimated recovery time. In addition, I apprised them that I would not be sending Brandon back, even after his recovery period, unless and until they took measures to help protect him. The principal contacted the Department of Public Safety regarding Brandon's non-attendance. However, he failed to apprise them that Brandon was at home, recovering from the brutal beating that had happened at their school. (Under Oklahoma law, the DPS could suspend a student's driver's license for non-attendance.) I had already researched the state law and knew that it was discretionary as to whether or not the school notified the Department of Public Safety. If the student had good cause for non-attendance, no notification was necessary. Being brutally beaten, in the school cafeteria, and recovering from surgery as a result thereof, apparently *didn't* meet our district's criteria for just cause.

So, while still at home recovering, Brandon walked out to our mailbox to find notification that he had to surrender his driver's license because he wasn't in school.

Then, with Oklahoma's failure to compel laws, the superintendent notified the district attorney's office that I was failing to compel my child to attend school. I had to get my attorney to call the prosecutor off. In addition, we had to submit numerous documents to the state Department of Public Safety for Brandon to keep his driver's license. While trying to help my child heal, and research his possible education alternatives, my time was being consumed with putting out the many fires the school was starting. It seemed that my actions to help protect my son had angered the school, so they utilized the state laws to victimize the victim and punish both Brandon and me.

On Dec. 16, 2000, Brandon put a loaded gun to his head, pulled the trigger and ended his pain.

Some of the bullies have said (through their crocodile tears), that they didn't realize what they were doing — that they were "just having fun." During those years, that they were just having fun, I had seen the sparkling light of joy, love, and hope in Brandon's big, beautiful, brown eyes slowly replaced with the darkness of pain, devastation and hopelessness. While they were "just having fun," I had watched my son die a slow and painful death.

One night, as Brandon stood by me, he said, "I feel dead inside." On a cold December morning, only three weeks later, I was standing by Brandon's dead body, knowing, that despite all my efforts to save my beloved son, the bullies' job had been done too well. Their mission had been accomplished. Suffice it to say that through all this, Brandon and all of us who love him were not "having fun."

Where was any justice for Brandon? Where is justice for us? Our light, our hope, our joy has been replaced with darkness, hopelessness, and an unrelenting sorrow. Now, we feel "dead inside."

As tragic as all of these deaths are, the greater tragedy is if society does not stop to look at the reasons, and pause for a moment to see "all the victims."

To Brandon

They came from the darkness like thieves in the night
They robbed us of our treasure as they stole your precious life

An arsenal of viciousness from deep within their hearts
Day by day, bit by bit they took your life apart

How were you to defend yourself or take back the life they stole
For you possessed no weapons in the repository of your soul

As they took your joy, your peace of mind and all your precious things
I wonder if these thieves did know they'd give you angel wings

May you rest in peace, and may others see what all your loved ones know
For they stole from all - when they robbed this earth
of your kind and gentle soul

Author, "Brandon's Mom"

The Aftermath
By Brandon's mom, Cathy Swartwood Mitchell

Justice was not to be had, not for Brandon or his loved ones left behind. Although I had difficulty finding an attorney who would take the case, Brandon and I had filed a lawsuit after he was brutally beaten in the school cafeteria. Regarding the attorneys, their reluctance was not a belief that Brandon had not been injured, or that he did not deserve compensation for his injuries and suffering, or even that the school should not be held responsible along with the student perpetrators. It was because the laws were not on our side. I would tell the attorneys what had happened: how Brandon was called faggot, pussy and little bitch day-in and day-out; how Brandon was threatened and assaulted; and how one of the perpetrators didn't like a shirt Brandon wore in the 8th grade, so he called Brandon a Satanist, for years, as he would knock him in the head or shove him into lockers.

Then the attorneys would ask, "Is he?"

"Is he what?"

"Is he gay or a Satanist?"

"No, he is not," I would answer.

"Are you sure?"

I would then have to explain, "To the contrary, he has always had girlfriends, has had no gay tendencies and has even volunteered to mow the church grounds for several years."

The attorneys would respond with things like, "Well, with your documentation, if he were gay or a Satanist, you would have a multi-million dollar federal lawsuit. However, since he is not gay or a Satanist, his civil rights have not been violated. It would just be a state-level suit. With the tort reform in Oklahoma, there is a cap on what you can sue a school district or a municipality for. It's a max of one hundred thousand dollars per incident."

In disbelief, I would ask, "His civil rights haven't been violated? Doesn't my son have a right to go to school and get his education without being tormented, assaulted over and over and, then, brutally beaten?"

The attorneys would tell me that, technically, "Yes." However, it was not a federal civil rights violation unless it was over race, religion, sexual orientation or gender, etc. and that they were not willing to take on a school district for a max of a one-hundred-thousand-dollar judgment.

Brandon was an intelligent, white, heterosexual, Christian male. He had no disabilities, other than in the aftermath and because of the bullies' actions.

Finally, we were referred to an attorney who took the case. He told me that the requirements to sue a school district under Oklahoma law were stringent and the time frame of incidents that we could sue for was very limited. He said, "The school had to be able to reasonably foresee that injuries would occur to Brandon, yet did nothing to prevent it." We had the documentation of notification, which was shrugged off by school administrators over and over again, and five-thousand dollars in medical bills for surgery after Brandon was beaten in the school cafeteria. In addition, Brandon still had difficulty breathing through his nose after the attack.

The surgery had (mostly) fixed him externally, but internally the damage could not be undone.

The attorney filed the lawsuit including three incidents that fell under time-frame restrictions and which also met the notification criteria under state law, resulting in a total of a three-hundred-thousand dollar lawsuit.

The school eventually filed for dismissal of the lawsuit. The system is slow, and over a year had passed (since the beating) before Brandon got a hearing date in court. There had been much happen in that year. I had pulled Brandon from school, never letting him go back after he was beaten. It was a decision that made Brandon somewhat upset with me. Brandon was a strong, stubborn child. He had always asserted that "they" were not going to make him run and that he had a right to go to school. It made my decision that much harder, especially when he would argue, "Why do I have to leave school and live with the stigma of being a high-school dropout, when I did nothing wrong?" Nonetheless, Brandon obtained his GED and enrolled in a local community college.

Brandon was also struggling with PTSD, (Post Traumatic Stress Disorder), exhibiting many symptoms. He was sleep-deprived and had uncontrollable trembling at the slightest reminders of the incidents and the perpetrators. Brandon was angry, frustrated and began self-medicating with marijuana. We had sought psychological treatment, and for a while, Brandon was on an anti-depressant. He attempted suicide, by jumping his four-wheeler off a steep bank into the swift moving currents of the Arkansas River, only six months before he completed suicide with the gun. (Brandon loved his four-wheeler. He left a suicide note that time too. We took his attempt seriously and admitted him to a facility for several weeks until the psychiatrist determined that he was no longer a threat to himself.)

On one trip home from the attorney's office, Brandon was trembling and angry; we had both given sworn statements for a hearing. It was hard for Brandon to relive it all. He told me more than once that he just wanted to forget. Yet, at other times, he and I had an overwhelming need to seek justice or some semblance thereof. As a mother, I was confused and torn.

We attended a hearing before a judge two days before Thanksgiving of 2000.

During the hearing, Brandon and I had to listen to false allegations from the school's attorney. One of our claims was that the principal had torpedoed our attempt to transfer Brandon to another school district, prior to the attack in the cafeteria. Their attorney said that I had not pursued the transfer. That was a lie. The transfer was denied. The principal's wife was interim superintendent at the district we were trying to transfer Brandon to . . . Then there were insinuations from their attorney of how Brandon must have done something to deserve what he got. Nothing specific, just it "must have" been his fault. At one point, I remember her saying something like, "Come on your honor. He's having trouble with three of them." I guess their attorney thought that the perpetrators running in a pack, like wild dogs, attacking my child, added weight to the school's argument that Brandon must have done something to make *three* guys want to do this to him. (School administrators asked us that on numerous occasions, even though the perpetrators were telling the school things like "We just don't like him" and "I think he's a Satanist because he wore a shirt in the eighth grade that said...")

We were not allowed to say anything during the hearing. It consisted of the attorneys arguing to the judge. I was not very happy about our attorney being unprepared when responding to the "transfer" issue, in addition to several other issues. The judge dismissed the claim regarding the transfer; however, the major portion of the lawsuit held up. The judge ruled that we had a right to have a jury hear our case. I remember him telling the school's attorney that under Oklahoma law, it was a question of "notification" from us to the school and that I had "notified" the school of the problems.

During the arguments in court that day, Brandon got very upset at the allegations from the school's attorney. He began trembling and quietly got up and walked out of the courtroom. About ten minutes later, the judge ruled and I went out to the bench outside the door where Brandon was sitting. I could tell that he was not doing well. I told him that we had won this round, but that if pursuing this were going to hurt him more than help him, we would drop the lawsuit. Brandon said, "No, Mom. I want them held accountable."

Shortly thereafter, Brandon began another spiral downward and three weeks later, he was dead. During those three weeks, much happened; we talked on many occasions. I told him that it appeared as though he had gone into self-destruct mode. I asked him to let me call the psychotherapist and make an appointment for him. He refused. He knew that I was thinking about committing him to a facility for treatment for depression. Brandon told me to forget it and said, "If you do, I promise you I will go in a body bag or I will come out in one." He also promised me that he wouldn't attempt suicide again. He kept saying, "I'll be all right Mom."

December 16, 2000 my son broke his promise to me. He left a note . . . A one-page note putting everything in order: who should get what of his belongings, thanking some people for good things they had done, telling his friends "I cared about you all and I'm sorry, but none of you would have ever changed my mind." He told his girlfriend that he loved her and had some final words for his family, "I love you Mom, Dad and Daniel. I am sorry I left you."

Brandon also had some things to say about why he put the gun to his head, "I would be going through none of this if it weren't for how I was treated in High School." Then he names an administrator and three of the student perpetrators, saying they, "...need to pay for what they did and my soul will not rest till they do."

That was the first time I heard the word "pay" versus "held accountable" from Brandon when referring to seeking justice. He had told me in one of our final conversations, "Mom, the school system didn't work, the police department didn't work and the courts don't work. The system doesn't work and it's never going to change and you can't tell me that it will."

After Brandon's death, our attorney told me that the "complexion of the case had changed." He said that instead of a multiple incident personal injury case, we now had a single incident wrongful death case - a maximum of one-hundred-thousand dollars. I was appalled with the fact that even if we were successful and received a judgment for what had happened to Brandon, it would cost the school less with Brandon dead than alive.

Months later, we received a letter from the attorney for the school to our attorney. It said, "This case has been pending for some time . . . Further, I understand that Brandon Swartwood is now deceased. Nevertheless, I have been instructed by my client to offer the sum of $1,500 to fully, and finally, settle this case. Please convey this offer to your client, and let me know her response within the next ten (10) days."

I told my attorney what they could do with their offer. A few months later, my attorney told me that it was not "economically feasible" for him to pursue the case.

The first thing I did was attend a school board meeting. Among other things, I read the letter from their attorney offering fifteen hundred dollars "to fully and finally settle this..." I told them that they might consider fifteen hundred dollars a generous offer, but I considered it an insult. I told them that my first thought was, "They helped kill him...I guess they think it sufficient to help pay for disposing of his body." I told them that my child mattered and that all these kids matter. "So thank you, but no thank you." I also told them that this would never "fully and finally" be settled. Then I told them that I had good news and bad news. "The good news is that I am dropping the suit against this school and it's not going to cost you a dime." I followed with, "The bad news is I no longer must remain silent."

I had no idea what I was going to do after that. I just blurted it out. Maybe it was a God-thing. I walked out of the meeting, collapsed to the sidewalk, as I said to my mother, "I don't know why I said that." I had said plenty during the 45 minutes that I had the floor. That was one of the mildest statements I made that night, yet it was the one that ran through my mind over and over. I did a lot of praying, asking God what my place was in all of this. It would be a while before I would have my answer. In the meantime, Brandon's statement, about his soul not resting, haunted me. I knew that there was no hope of justice, from the courts anyway, for my son.

Our family has struggled with anger and depression since Brandon's death. I had PTSD - The image of my child lying there (without getting graphic, he used a .357 Magnum), is forever etched in my mind. I struggle to keep that image from appearing every time I look at a picture of my son. Other family members didn't get to say their goodbyes to Brandon.

We had his body cremated and used a picture at the memorial service.

For several years, I tried to work. I had no focus, no energy and enough anger to do a mass killing of those responsible. Thank God, I had enough maturity, morals and maintained enough sanity, barely, to refrain from seeking revenge. I say "barely" on the sanity thing because I was crazy with grief and anger. With the PTSD, sleep deprivation and my mind racing when I should have been resting, I started to justify seeking revenge. Sometimes, a thought of what I would like to do, would progress into a plan. It would go step by step, frame by frame, like a video tape with no off button. I would bang my head on the arm of the sofa to try to get the thoughts to stop. I was sleeping so little, the sofa is where I stayed for several years, with the television going all night long. I thought if I could watch something then I wouldn't see the video playing in my head. It didn't work. I had a whole set of revenge tapes that played without warning, no pause or stop button. Mentally, I was tortured.

I would argue with myself, that I would not let them take my soul. Brandon hadn't. He had a gun and bullets and he fired but one. Oftentimes, I thought about doing that too. Then I thought about the pain that it would cause my loved ones and I couldn't do that either. It wasn't an argument that I won in one night. It took years to fully accept that living and letting others live was my only true choice.

Grieving is a process, and for me it has been a very long one. I literally became disabled. Brandon's father was struggling too. It is hard to go out and try to conquer the world every day, when we could not save our own child. We had to sell our home.

After Brandon's death, I had read that about 85% of couples who lose a child, divorce. We became a statistic after 29 years of marriage. Our son, Daniel, lost his brother and his best friend, he lost his parents emotionally for several years, he lost his home and then he saw his parents' divorce. Unfortunately, that was only the beginning of the aftermath.

Shortly before Brandon died, he had made reference to the thought that he was causing his family too much trouble and costing us too much money. I told him that we would sell the house, if we needed to, to help him. We had spent thousands on medical bills and therapy. Somehow, Brandon felt badly that "he" was costing us all that money. I honestly think that he justified, in his mind, leaving us by telling himself that we would all be better off. I still believe that if anyone involved, including the school, had stepped up to the plate, accepted responsibility for their actions and negligence, and quit blaming the victim, Brandon would have survived. I think that in the end he believed that something was wrong with him and someway, somehow, he must be to blame.

Brandon wasn't to blame. That statement about, "no longer remaining silent," and my prayers about where my place was in all of this, finally came together in a one-word answer: Awareness. It was so simple, yet it took so long for it to register.

I had written a memoriam on the first anniversary of Brandon's death that was far from traditional. The publisher of the local paper refused to print it and according to his editor "wouldn't print anything that Cathy Swartwood says or writes." Politics! ...Everyone covering for everyone else and returning favors. Locally, they had swept his death under the rug. If they had their way, I would be silenced like the victims of bullying. The only difference was that I was dealing with adult bullies in positions of power.

As I sat there crying, feeling helpless that I could not even get a paid memoriam printed locally, I picked the phone up and called the Tulsa newspaper office. They asked me to fax the memoriam and they printed it. The circulation was well over 100 times that of the local paper, in addition many locals read the Tulsa paper. By trying to silence me, they had just given me a louder, stronger voice.

I had done some writing about what had happened to my son. I sent Brandon's story to Senator Rozell, in support of an anti-bullying bill that he had introduced into the Senate in Oklahoma. Senator Rozell is a former school principal. The bill became law. *NBC Nightly News with Tom Brokaw* aired a segment about the new law. Included in the segment were pictures of Brandon and an interview with me about how Brandon had been bullied to death.

The next year, I wrote a poem to Brandon. A new newspaper had just started publishing in Coweta, so I took the poem to them. The publisher and the editor both read it and told me they would print it. They didn't. They didn't even bother calling me so that I could submit it to another publication for printing on the second anniversary of Brandon's death. After corresponding with the publisher, I mailed a commentary, along with the poem and all the correspondence, to 150 local businesses. I just wanted the locals to know the facts before they spent their advertising dollars. The paper folded within months. I also e-mailed the poem to Brenda High and she posted it on her website, JaredStory.com, where Brandon's story was also posted. The *Dr. Phil Show* ran across it and called me. Daniel and I were on a plane within days and taping a show. After the show aired, in an email to me, a producer wrote, "We are all proud of that show and you did an exceptional job in making people *aware*. We received over 700,000 comments on our website the day the show aired." In addition, the show was voted the third most popular show of the season by Dr. Phil viewers. Once again, in trying to silence me, the locals had inadvertently empowered me. I finally understood why I had said what I did in that school board meeting and what the one-word answer to my prayers, "Awareness" meant.

I still struggle with depression and grief. I miss Brandon. The injustice is a pill that I still cannot swallow. None of the perpetrators ever had charges filed against them for the crimes they committed against my son. However, at least three of them have had numerous felony charges or convictions for some of their other crimes. Those same three have had protective orders filed against them by their spouses or girlfriends. Their charges range from possession of a controlled substance and multiple burglaries, to domestic abuse and child abuse. As students, they were liars, thieves, thugs and abusers. Now, these school bullies, in adulthood, are society's criminals.

I had researched the statistics and knew what kind of men these thugs would probably become. As a result, I followed some of their court proceedings over the past 6 years. One of the repeat offenders (I'll refer to him as "Pete" as a result of his re'peat' offenses) has alone been charged with: Unlawful possession of controlled drug, Unlawful possession of controlled substance, Domestic abuse, Malicious injury to property, Driving under suspension, (then another) Domestic Assault and Battery, and last but not least, Child abuse by injury. As of this writing, Pete has just had another protective order filed against him by the recipient of his domestic abuse. (I, too, filed a protective order against Pete, on Brandon's behalf in March of 1999, which was never enforced by local authorities)

Pete stalked my son for years. He harassed and assaulted my son on many occasions. Brandon wasn't Pete's only target during those years in school. Pete left many victims in his wake and spent much time in the Alternative Ed program at the school. School officials tried to sweep the incidents, with the other victims, under the rug and continued to ask Brandon what he was doing to make Pete target him. I believe I know the answer. Brandon was very intelligent, insightful, nice looking, hard working, considerate and well rounded. Above all, Brandon had a gentle soul. Brandon was everything that Pete was not and could never be.

After Brandon's death, an employee involved in the Alternative Ed program at the school, called me. She told me there were some things that I should know, that Pete had many victims. She said that Pete was very violent and the school was fully aware. Pete was big enough to do damage, as he was 5'11" and 200 plus pounds. (Brandon was 5'9" and 145 pounds.) She said that she and others in the school were personally afraid of Pete; however, the directive, as instructed by school officials, was "to get Pete eligible to play football again."

I was incensed. The school administrators knew how violent Pete was all along, yet furthering Pete's football career and enhancing their football program was more important to them than my child's safety or education, and ultimately, Brandon's life.

My child died...Pete dropped out of school. It appears as though the closest thing Pete has to a career is committing crimes and going to court. Proper intervention might have saved them both. I know it would have saved Brandon.

Several years ago, out of curiosity, I went to one of Pete's court appearances. Pete received a slap on the wrist, an insignificant punishment, for a domestic abuse charge. It appears that with all the charges, Pete had received probation or suspended or deferred sentences, with minimal fines.

After the proceedings, while still in the courtroom, I approached Pete as he and his mother were laughing and chatting. Pete did not recognize me. I calmly asked Pete if I could see his hands. He complied. I took both of his hands in mine. I turned them palm up, then palm down as I quietly studied them. Pete stood there, somewhat puzzled. Then I looked him squarely in his eyes and said, "I just wanted to see if you still had Brandon Swartwood's blood on your hands. You do...and you will never be able to wash it off."

Pete reacted as if I had threatened his life. He stepped back, looking fearful, and started yelling, "She, uh, she, uh, uh, she said . . ." His mother then chimed in stammering as she tried to summon Pete's attorney.

Pete's attorney ran over questioning what had happened. While Pete and his mother continued to stammer, I relayed what I had said to Pete. His attorney told me that I had no right to say that. I disagreed. (I believe that my dead child, and Pete's part in his death, gave me every right to say what I did.) In short, Pete's attorney told me that I needed to leave the courtroom. I refused, so he stepped outside the door and returned with a deputy. I, then, voluntarily walked outside the courtroom with the deputy and the prosecutor. While I was telling the prosecutor what I thought of the justice system in the county, we continued to walk down the hall and then outside. As we exited, I was surprised at the number of people waiting, around the courthouse steps, for court appearances. While still talking, the prosecutor and I walked past them and on down to the sidewalk.

When we reached the sidewalk, the prosecutor left and two other men approached me. They had heard some of the discussion with the prosecutor regarding the lack of justice for my child. In a failed attempt to calm me, one of the men said, "My son was murdered and I can't get them to file any charges either."

Rather than calming me, his statement had the opposite effect. I shouted, "That's supposed to make me feel better? You tell me that your son was murdered and they won't file any charges for that either?" The men told me to calm down and I continued with, "I am supposed to calm down, knowing that there is no justice, period, in this county?"

At that point, a deputy in uniform approached me saying, "You have no right to be here." Being disagreeable that day, I disagreed with him too. Next thing I know, the deputy is telling me to "tell it to the judge" as he grabs my right arm. Simultaneously, the other two men, who were then behind me, pounced me. I turned, jerking my left arm from them. They grabbed me again, while the deputy clutched my right arm. The three of them maintained their holds as they all manhandled me back up the steps and into the courthouse. (I was not resisting. I'm 5'7" and 125 pounds. Nonetheless, I guess they thought it necessary for all three of them to "help" me to the jail cell.) I believed that all I had done was voice my opinion in public—loud enough for the public to hear. However, the deputy was threatening me with charges of assaulting an officer and resisting arrest. The next thing I knew, I was in the cell with the door slamming shut.

Come to find out, one of the two men who had been talking to me was the Under-Sheriff in plain clothes. I hadn't noticed the badge on his belt or the gun. I had jerked (and slung my arm according to them) as he grabbed me. They were threatening to turn that into a charge of assaulting an officer. As to the resisting arrest, I was never told to leave the sidewalk or that I was under arrest. All I was told by the deputy, before the three of them grabbed me, was that I didn't have a right to be there.

During the commotion, on the sidewalk, I had caught a glimpse of Pete and his mother watching and smirking as they walked to their car. I was shocked and humiliated by what was happening. Pete had never served one minute in jail for the crimes against my son and yet, I was being thrown in a jail cell for talking too loudly. For a brief moment, I was able to lock eyes with Pete and in frustration and anger I yelled, "Brandon should have put the bullet in your head!"

So there I sat, for the first time in my life, in jail. I had a prescription bottle of pills in my jean jacket. I was an emotional wreck. I emptied the entire bottle into my hand as I contemplated my situation. I was sitting there, with the pills in my hand and the empty prescription bottle laying beside me on the cot, when a jailer walked by, looked in the window and saw the bottle. She stepped in, picked up the empty bottle, and then told me that I was not allowed to have those in there. She stepped back out and locked the door. I sat there, in disbelief that she had not inquired as to where the contents of the bottle were. I was sitting in a jail cell, crying, depressed and distraught with a hand-full of potentially lethal pills.

I slid from the cot to the floor and sat down behind the solid door. I positioned myself far away from the side glass, where they couldn't observe me. As I sat there, I then thought about the irony of the situation. God knows my sense of humor and He knew that I would have to live to tell this one. It was about an hour before they came back to the cell and released me (without filing any charges).

I don't regret going to the courthouse that day. I don't regret shedding light on the darkness of injustice. In addition, I will never regret utilizing my voice for my silenced child, regardless of the punishment I receive.

I will continue to speak out and fulfill my place in all this. I have received hundreds of emails and letters from "Brandon's Story" (www.jaredstory.com/brandon.html). While most have been from victims or parents needing help, or adult survivors who still suffer the scars, many have been from educators who acknowledge the problem and are taking a proactive approach to address the bullying epidemic.

Of all the correspondence I have received, one sums up my feelings about the magnitude of the injustice that Brandon suffered. A marine, also named Brandon, emailed me. The marine offered his condolences and then his understanding, when he closed with, ". . . we know who really pulled the trigger."

Yes, Brandon - Yes, we do.

Cathy's postscripts...

P.S. I have since managed to stay out of jail. (I moved to another county.)

P.S.S. The District Attorney, in the meantime, has been indicted, by a multi county grand jury, for embezzlement. As of this writing, he is free on bond awaiting trial. His office manager was indicted for perjury along with one of his former prosecutors. The prosecutor was also charged with possession of a controlled drug and offering false evidence. Both the office manager and the prosecutor pleaded guilty to their charges and have been placed on probationary sentences. The grand jurors wrote, "The district attorney's office should serve as a minister of justice, rather than one who facilitates standards of conduct which fall beneath the character of law abiding citizens." It goes on to say that the district attorney, "created his own nest of deception and thievery" and responded with expressions of "scorn and contempt" for individuals responsible for bringing the events to light.

"Fighting the System"

"It's your child. You must fight for him or her. No one cares like a parent cares - a parent is motivated by love."

Jared's Story
The Scars Never Go Away

In loving memory of
Jared Benjamin High
09/23/85 – 09/29/98
By Brenda High

The day that changed my life
At 10 a.m. on Sept. 29, 1998, I received a phone call from emergency services. They said to come home — my husband was there...and he needed me. That's all they would say.

As I came in the door, Bill, my husband, was sitting motionless in our kitchen chair. In a low, sad voice, he said, "Brenda, Jared's shot himself. He's dead." ...I collapsed to my knees at my husband's chair, burying my head in Bill's lap. I began to cry. Jared was just 13 years and 6 days old. That was the moment, the day that changed my life forever.

Nothing could ever be the same again. Our gift was taken from us. We would not have the treasured joy and responsibility of raising our youngest child to adulthood.

When a police officer asked me, "Why would Jared do such a thing?" I answered flatly, "He's never been the same since he was beat up at school."

It is small consolation, but it is funny the things you think about as you try to wrap your mind around such unimaginable things as the suicide of your own child. In my grief, I felt "lucky". Unlike other parents who search for years asking "why?", at least I had that answer. I knew why.

A little about Jared
When Jared was a baby, he had frequent ear infections. This repetitive problem caused him to develop speech problems. He was different from other children. So different in fact that he attended high school at age three, well, his special speech class was at a high school.

What Jared could not manage with words he made up for in physical ability. He began climbing doorjambs and hallway walls when he was about one and a half. On the first day of his speech class, I received a frantic call from one of the teachers to "come quick, Jared has climbed the fence and won't come down!"

When I arrived, Jared was already down, but I told the teachers, "Oh, don't worry, that fence is only 12 feet tall – he'll be fine." I think Jared enjoyed making people "ooh" and "aah" at his amazing physical abilities.

As Jared grew, he didn't talk much. However, he used his talent for physical sports to make many friends. By the time he was 9 or 10, his verbal skills were fine. Unfortunately, these speech delays caused Jared to get behind in school.

Jared was a quiet, reserved and gentle boy by nature. He loved animals and people. He was always more concerned about others than himself. When he saw someone who looked hungry on the street, he would ask if we could take him a McDonald's hamburger. That's just the kind of sensitive child he was.

In his spare time, he enjoyed exploring, jumping on the trampoline; playing in his rickety, homemade tree house, watching "The Simpsons", or playing with one of his two best friends, Brian or Jonathan. If it was fun and/or physical, Jared wanted to do it. He was able to make friends by excelling physically, in spite of his speech problems.

The Assault – *All of this information was retrieved off an audio tape taken from an "investigation" of the assault by the insurance representative of the Pasco School District. Jared was interviewed, but to our knowledge, the bully never was.*

Jared was a sixth grader when he experienced bullying for the first time. It began when he volunteered as team manager (a.k.a. the coach's water boy) for the eighth grade baseball team. Jared enjoyed working with the coach, but did not like some of the boys who played on the team. Four or five of these boys thought it was entertaining to spit sunflower seeds at Jared, and to chase and kick him. They stole his prized baseball glove that he had since he was in T-ball and anything else they could tell was important to him.

After enduring nearly a full season of torment, the bullying came to a head on Wednesday, May 6, when Jared went inside his middle school gym to make a phone call. After hanging up the phone, Jared took a few steps forward before noticing that Brutus* had come into the gymnasium. (*I will call the bully "Brutus," after a famous 'back-stabbing' Roman historical figure.) Brutus was the meanest, most accomplished, and determined bully in the school.

Jared began to walk toward the hallway door and looked at Brutus briefly, giving him what Jared later called, "the evil eye." At that point, Brutus stopped my son by grabbing his shirt. After looking around to be sure no adults were present, Brutus asked Jared, "What are you going to do about it now?" ("It" of course meant being alone with no one to help him). Jared later commented to an insurance investigator for the Pasco School District that at this point he knew he "was about to get beat up."

Brutus commenced his brutal assault by picking Jared up and throwing, as well as pushing Jared against the walls. As Jared fell to the ground, Brutus then kicked and punched him in the stomach and shoulders. Several times Jared yelled for help calling, "Teacher, Teacher!" But no one came to his aid.

I should mention that Brutus was a very large eighth grader. Some have referred to him as "fat, with muscles". He weighed at least 175 pounds. Jared, on the other hand, was two years younger, weighed 98 pounds, and was almost six inches shorter than Brutus. It was not the first time this bully had assaulted a younger or smaller child; Brutus had a history of this type of behavior and had, in at least one incident, been reported to the police.

Brutus assaulted Jared for approximately eight minutes. Knowing there was no one around to save Jared, he 'came back' several times, once after getting a drink of water and attempting to dump out Jared's backpack, and continued to brutalize him.

When Jared was able to escape to the outside of the building, Brutus followed him outside and threw him against a brick wall a few more times, causing the back of his hand to bleed. Brutus' friends witnessed this last part of the assault and, as gang members usually do, they backed their leader and did nothing to stop the assault.

When questioned by investigators about this incident, Brutus' friends labeled Jared a "wimp", deserving of the beating he got. As is always the case, this is an indefensible position. Of course, Jared bore no fault. Only in a immature teenager or child's mind could believe that being smaller, or younger, or different, would mean that one is 'deserving' of a beating.

Jared wore an imaginary target on his back, as so many, if not all kids do.

Jared did not do anything to deserve the attack. But a bully, unchecked and ignored by school officials, will not stop bullying; he will take aim at his targets and make them his victims, simply because he/she can. It's not a new dynamic.

Brutus threatened Jared several times with promises that he was going to kill him, during this attack and later, in front of Jared's brother and Brutus' friends. The school officials never took any of these threats seriously. I often wonder if this assault and threat had taken place after the Columbine shootings, in April 1999. Would the school officials have paid more attention? It is a sad and hopeless thing for me to contemplate, that the death of many teenagers in that one incident may have saved my child's life. Possibly simple *timing* could have been the key factor in determining Jared's fate.

The day of that vicious attack, when Jared's older brother came to pick him up from school, my younger was crying. Jared's brother confronted Brutus, which soon drew the attention of adults at the school. It had been estimated that more than 20 minutes went by before any adults asked any questions about what happened. Disgustingly, the school officials were more concerned that Jared's brother had become involved, than the original assault.

The next day, unbeknownst to his father and me until later, Jared was interrogated by a vice principal with no parent or adult there to help him answer to his abuser. He interviewed both the bully and the victim in the same room. Jared hardly said a word. After all, Brutus had threatened to kill him the day before.

In fear of retribution and for his life, Jared said the assault was partially his fault. Because he gave Brutus the "evil eye," he deserved to be brutally beaten by him. He was too intimidated to bring up the atmosphere of fear and violence that Brutus had created. Jared was being intimidated and threatened by a bully twice his size, nearly a hundred pounds heavier, but the vice principal did not care. He suspended both Jared and the bully from school for three days for "fighting."

I did not find out about this entire event (the attack, the interrogation) until returning from a business trip the next day.

Two days after the beating, on Friday (May 8), I filed a police report with a county deputy and asked them to press charges against Brutus. I was grateful that the county deputy classified the incident as an "assault."

A visit to the chiropractor compared Jared's before-the-assault X-ray, (taken in early February 1998), to his after-the-assault X-ray and remarked, "It looks like he's been through a major car accident!" The chiropractor concluded that if Jared had been thrown against a wall one more time, he might have had his neck broken and died.

We also took Jared to his regular family physician where he confirmed that Jared's repeated vomiting was most likely caused from punches or kicks to the stomach.

During the summer of 1998, Jared began to struggle with noises in his head and sleeping problems. I knew that Jared was not the same, but I was uneducated about the signs of depression and felt Jared was going through some sort of Post Traumatic Stress Disorder, like soldiers who cannot seem to recuperate from battle experiences.

Yes, I was angry with the bully who hurt Jared, but most of all I blamed the administrators at the school. I felt that by the school's actions (or lack thereof), they were telling Jared that he deserved what happened to him. In the end, I believe it was really out of laziness and insensitivity to the seriousness of bullying that the school felt that one child's safety and self-esteem were not worth their efforts.

The school district refused to take any responsibility; that was a financial and legal decision. They were determined not to have to pay Jared's chiropractic and medical bills. In addition to constant frustration, I was also concerned for my son's mental state. How would a young boy feel when he realizes that the adults who are supposed to be there to protect him don't really care after all? How could he feel safe? And how can he learn and grow in that environment?

A few months after the assault, Brutus was told by juvenile authorities to go to anger management class at the high school for what he had done to Jared...a small, but hollow victory.

Jared received a letter from the juvenile authorities telling him that he was a victim and that they were sorry. He received no counseling from his middle school for his emotional injuries, no help for his physical injuries, and no apologies. Although the juvenile authorities did acknowledge his plight, from the school district he received just two things--blame and denial. No help.

Why is it that bullies will get counseling for bullying, but the victim is left on their own, with no allies, to struggle with low self-esteem, depression, and a feeling of worthlessness? The irony was striking to me.

When I realized that the school district had refused to investigate any further (after only one statement lasting about 20 minutes from Jared, and no interview with Brutus), and they would not take responsibility for their ongoing negligence where Brutus' well-known behavior was concerned, we decided to transfer Jared into a different school district. We believed a new start would help him. Perhaps solve the problem.

At the conclusion of Jared's first day in his new school, Hanford Middle School, he raved about how great the school was and how nice the kids were. We relaxed. That was a BIG mistake. We incorrectly believed that everything was okay, and that Jared would go back to his old self. But sadly, depression doesn't go away that easily; we were ignorant of the effect the chronic bullying had on his self-esteem.

The day that changed my life came on a Tuesday morning, not long after he transferred to the new school. Jared refused to go to school that day, and refused to talk to me. After I left for work, he went into my office — where I type this story right now — and picked up my phone. He called his father and said, "Dad … Dad, I just called to say goodbye" and then he shot himself, dying instantly. *(Please read, "Judging the Method's of Suicide" in the Special Submissions section for more information on the use of a gun in suicides.)*

No one can possibly describe the emotional and physical pain our family experienced on that day, and for weeks, months, and even years to come. Words cannot speak of the confusion, the anger, the hurt, the love, yes, the love we have felt. I believe the intensity of the pain one feels after a loved one dies equals the intensity of love one felt for that person when they lived. Oh, how we loved that boy, and I know that my husband and I would have done anything, forfeited our own lives, to save him, had we known the situation was that dire.

When someone you love dies, especially a child, it feels like a gaping, bleeding wound has opened up in your heart. It is not the natural order of things; to outlive your children; to lose a child in the manner we did. You think you will never stop hurting. However, in a few months for some, and in a few years for others, the wound begins to heal. A huge emotional scar forms. At first, the scar hurts to the touch. Just hearing your child's name or recalling a memory makes the scar throb with pain.

The scar never goes away. But with the passing of time, I can now touch my scar, and it doesn't hurt as it used to. After eight years, my scar has healed, in the sense that it is no longer visible. Healed...but the scar will never go away. And I don't want it to go away. I am proud that I have survived. My family has survived. We have found strength in each other and a cause greater than ourselves to work towards. Jared will always be an inspiration to us.

I believed on that terrible day in 1998 that I would never laugh again. But just two days after Jared died, my 72-year-old father and I walked out to the backyard and saw Jared's favorite pastime, his trampoline. My daughter, Sonja, had been coaxed into jumping on it by her cousin. Inspired by my son's memory, my dad and I both climbed on the trampoline and started jumping too. I felt guilty laughing, very guilty, but I laughed anyway. Seeing my 72-year-old father reviving Jared's spirit, that was the first realization for me that life does go on. That it must. It was a very confusing time, but I realized then that I could and would laugh again.

Losing a child is not the end of life. It is simply a profound change in life. It is a journey I did not choose, but one I am forced to take. I have discovered there is a key to how I survive the journey – I can CHOOSE my path towards healing, and HOW I will heal. Will I choose to be *bitter* road or will I choose to be *better* road? There is only one letter separating the two choices. That letter is "I." I was born an optimist. And I will die an optimist. "I" choose to be better.

Through the website I created as a tribute to Jared, (www.jaredstory.com), I have found peace and healing in expressing my thoughts about Jared, his short life, the bullying, his depression, and his suicide. JaredStory.com was my healing website, at least for the first few years. Now it has become a launching pad for the new path I have chosen.

I now find fulfillment in helping others to think about the effects of bullying on their own child, and in their own communities. I have successfully worked to enact legislation for victims of bullying and consequences for bullies. I have become a resource for other parents and mothers who are dealing with the same issues I dealt with several years ago. I am always hopeful that Jared's story might be the one (unforgettable) story that will help a parent prevent a similar fate for his or her own child.

If I could teach any lesson to those reading Jared's story, it would be to love your children each day; you never really know if they will be with you the next day...for whatever reason. Give them praise and hugs and encouragement and, finally, fight like hell for them if your school and community idly stand by while a bully takes away their spirit for living.

Looking Back – Looking Forward
10 Steps to Stop Bullying
By Jared's mom, Brenda High

Hindsight is not a pleasant experience for most parents who have had children bullied at school. We have all made mistakes when dealing with our schools over bullying incidents. The good news is that our mistakes can be your lessons, if you will apply them to your circumstances.

After Jared was bullied and then assaulted by one specific bully, he became more depressed. Before Jared took his life, we began a search for an attorney to take legal action against our school district for Jared's physical and psychological damages. However, an attorney who would represent a 12-year-old boy bullied in school was very hard to find. We didn't give up because we felt Jared's rights had been violated – the right to a safe and secure environment as well as other basic human rights – there was no doubt they had been violated. We searched diligently for a special attorney who would represent a young boy who was wronged by a bully and his school.

We were ready to secure an attorney we found in Seattle Washington, when Jared died. At that point, everything changed. The lawsuit became a "wrongful death" lawsuit instead of a suit for retribution, punishment and damages. We were fortunate enough to find two wonderful attorneys in Spokane, Washington, who would support our cause through a long legal process, over four years, and bring our case to a close.

In January 2003, eleven days before the planned trial was to begin, we settled our case. In my opinion, the money was almost nothing, $140,000 (much less after costs associated with Jared's death, deposition costs and attorneys fees), but the trial briefs that our attorney had prepared were worth their weight in gold. Those trial briefs have been the basis of advice, lessons, relayed warnings, writings, WebPages, and telephone conversations for the four years since the settlement. They have helped numerous parents and students fight the system and right the wrongs in their own school districts. School districts have learned lessons because of these briefs too...the main lesson – good record keeping is the key to the prevention of lawsuits.

Based on all the lessons we have learned, here are 10 steps that parents can take to stop the bullying in schools and reduce the effects of a child's suffering and victimization at the hands of a bully or bullies.

Step 1 – Does your child need medical treatment – Should you call the police?

First and foremost, if your child was injured or assaulted, get your child to a medical facility and have him/her checked out. Get a copy of the doctor's report and notes for your records. Then, if your child was injured, call the police and have a police report filed. Get a copy of this report too. Ask the police to press charges against the child who assaulted your child. In all honesty, they may balk at this plan of action. If they do, tell the police that your child has a constitutional right to have a police report filled out and added to their records, whether they do anything or not. What you really want is the record on file – who knows if the bully, who beat up your child, may become a career criminal and you want to do your part for justice, just in case.

Step 2 - Get the story

Conduct your own investigation. Find out from all sources what happened and write it down or record it. We learned from our own experiences that accurate documentation of all events is critical. Ask your child to be totally truthful about the events leading up to the bullying and the bullying or assault. Be aware that your child might be traumatized and may have a difficult time talking about what happened. Listen to your child with your heart and with your mind. Let your child know they have done the right thing by coming to talk to you and that you will find a way to help solve this problem.

If you find that your child did something to encourage or provoke the bully, record it. This does not mean your child deserved to be bullied, because no child deserves to be bullied, only that he/she may have made himself a target in the mind of the bully. This can be useful information to consider for behavioral changes that may help your child avoid such things in the future.

To put this in perspective, say you are an adult at work and someone you are uncomfortable with walks past you, and while they walk past, you give them "the evil eye" (as Jared gave to his bully). In a work environment, would that person have a right to beat you up? No. However, you may have given the bully a reason to choose you as a target.

Because of the emotionally unstable nature of some children, something as simple as an "evil eye" might set off an unusually angry or violent reaction, and might result in a disproportionate response. The bully is never, NEVER, right to hurt or assault his victim/target and the victim is never, NEVER at fault for being hurt or assaulted. We should note that for the sake of this discussion, we are not talking about an argument or fight between two inherently equal adolescents. We are talking about the unbalanced relationship between a bully and his/her victim. Nevertheless, since some children just seem to wear imaginary targets on their backs larger than other kids do, they must learn to minimize their risk of being victimized. They must learn behaviors that work (de-targeting skills), and avoid behaviors that don't. We teach our children not to run into traffic; we should do the same in this context.

Concerning the bully...when a bully has not been made to take responsibility for their actions, be it for bullying, retaliation, revenge, harassment, assault, and every other out-of-control activity, the bully will bully for any reason, and at any time. Parents, teachers and those who have an interest in the bully's welfare, need to insist that these aggressors take responsibility for their actions. To ignore this responsibility will lead to a life of irresponsible choices and possibly a criminal record for the bully.

Step 3 – Document everything
Although related to item 2 above, and mentioned therein, this bears repeating. Keep accurate notes and records. The process of documentation for bullying incidents is a parental responsibility that only ends when your child is no longer in your home. You must keep meticulous records, just as if you are the attorney representing your child. Ask your child to do the same. If you want to make it a fun exercise - grab a long handled spoon and pronounce on your child, "I now dub you a special junior attorney." Empower your child. Who knows, they may even become an attorney some day, or find a profession that utilizes such skills.

Conduct an interview with your child and then write down a synopsis in bullet points. If there were witnesses, get their statements and get signatures on those statements in front of an adult if they are a minor. Do not forget to add dates, names, times, who, what, when, where and why information you can find. Write down any comments made by administrators or teachers. These written notes may not seem like much at the time, but later, they may be a deciding point for justice in your child's favor. These records may aid in procedural changes that could dramatically reduce bullying in your school, and of your child.

In our case, I got the information from Jared, as well as some witnesses, but I didn't write all of it down. Consequently, I had to remember many of the details later, during interrogations and depositions. However, there was one comment by a Vice-Principal that I did write down, which came in handy later. When I asked the VP if he allows violent children to wander his halls stalking prey, particularly the bully who beat Jared up, he replied, "He's not that bad now, you should have seen him before he came to the middle school." That comment told me that this bully had a record of bullying other children, and the school knew it. That was valuable information. I was also able to do a lot more investigating because of that one comment.

Step 4 – Meet with the school
Think first, about how you will approach the school. If the school has no knowledge that your child is being bullied, then it is fair to give them a chance to deal with the bullying problem according to their guidelines. Give the school a reasonable timeframe, say a couple of days, to deal with the bullying problem, but let the school know you will be conducting your own investigation as well as following up to make sure the problem is being addressed. I really believe that most school administrators and teachers have a desire to have safe and bully-free schools. I hear many complaints of the bad schools because of the bullying prevention work I do. When you run an organization and website based on bullying, most of the news, unfortunately, is bad. So, go in with a positive attitude and give your school a chance to change things for your child. It is much more cost effective for a school to head-off a bullying issue than it is for them to wait until a serious crime has been committed (and perhaps a lawsuit comes their way). Communicate with your school about exactly that. Make them take the issue seriously.

Ask for a meeting with the administrator in charge of school safety and/or school discipline. In most cases that would be the Principal or one of the Vice-Principals. If you need emotional support or you have reason to believe that the meeting may be hostile, take a friend or adult relative with you as a witness. I once met with an administrator, alone, while I was a member of the school board. He made some sexually inappropriate comments that surprised me – I would have loved to have had a witness to that!

Let the administrator know that you will be keeping notes and that he/she will get a copy of the notes when you are able to type them. Why do we do this? The answer is that too often, reports of bullying seem to disappear like a sock in a washing machine. They get lost, never to be found again, unless, of course, the parent and the administrator keep a written record, a paper trail. Make sure they have a copy.

A little side comment – Under the *No Child Left Behind Act* a school's records will indicate whether the school is a safe school or a violent school. Federal and State Funds are passed out based on these records. The prestige and financial viability of the school may also be at risk here. There are many schools, dare I say, even the majority of schools, who "under report" incidents at their schools because they do not feel the incident was "big" enough or important enough to include in those records. Therefore, we as parents must *help* our schools be totally honest. Where your children are concerned, we must provide our schools with records and make their work easier, and honest.

Bullying happens mostly IN (and around) schools, and the administrators and teachers in our schools are the first line of prevention. However, if the schools will not do their jobs to protect children, parents can implement additional steps (see 9 and 10 below) to help protect their children, as well as other children, from further bullying. These days, schools are well aware of their legal responsibility to our children.

During the meeting(s), you want to accomplish these things:
- Get a copy of the school anti bullying policies
- Find out what anti bullying programs are being used
- Report your child's bullying experience and give copies of your statements/records to the administrator
- You want to be sure that the word is out about the bully and that there will be some consequences for his behavior
- You want your child in counseling – emotional damages can be lifelong
- Find common ground on what will be done to stop the bullying in the future
- If the bullying is happening in a particular classroom, ask for a daily update from the teacher
- Ask for a phone call from the principal within 48 hours, to report what has been done to help your child
- Talk about disagreements in a civil verbal exchange
- Be persistent and firm in your resolve

After the meeting with your administrator, again, type up the meeting minutes and send a copy to him/her for their records. If your meeting with the administrator was hostile or confrontational, make a note of it and send a copy of all your notes to the school superintendent and all members of your school board. Once you get the ball rolling with official documentation, in addition to feeling more compelled to resolve the issue, the school will recognize a legal obligation to act.

It is worth mentioning here that how the school decides to handle your child's case is critical. And you can assist in that process. Social standing is *everything* to a teenager. As was the case in Brandon's Story in this book, school administrators should be clearly instructed not to casually fraternize with, or otherwise involve the students in the details of the bullying issue when such communication will do further harm to the victim. That includes, what the school officials decide to share with other students and how they choose to address the bullying and direct students to eliminate it. These are critical decisions that require some expertise, finesse, and common sense. An anti bullying program or resource manual can help with such decisions.

Step 5 – Listen to your gut feelings

As a reminder, Jared was assaulted on a Wednesday afternoon, at the same time I was leaving town on a business trip.

On Thursday, Jared was kicked out of school for "fighting" and when I came back that evening, I was told what had happened.

On Friday, I took Jared to his Chiropractor and then to his Doctor. Then I went to the school to talk to the Principal. After talking to the principal, I believed Jared would not get justice, or the help he deserved from the school. I felt that the bully would hurt my child or other children again. The school asked me if they could handle this "fight" in-house, but, by continuing to deny that my child was the victim of an assault, I could see that they were not qualified to deal with my child's safety. After talking with the school, I came home and called the Sheriff's office to make out a report and press charges against the bully. A Deputy came to my home and made out the report calling the incident an assault, a clear case of assault, according to the officer.

On Saturday, I contacted a friend who was an attorney and asked him what I should do. Looking back to those first four days, the only mistake I made was to listen to his advice, as well intentioned as it was. What was his advice? He advised me to give the school time to handle the "incident" or "fight" as they called it, because he felt that the school "really did care" about my son. As the time wore on, in what seemed like slow motion, I found that that wasn't true in Jared's case. If only I had known. I realize now that though this advice was well intentioned, following it chipped away at the legal burden the school felt to protect my child. After all, if I wasn't firm in raising concerns about my child's health, then Jared must be okay. This was the wrong thing to do. I should have continued to apply pressure.

AGAIN - Listen to your gut feeling. If you have not been satisfied with the response you have received from School Administrators within a reasonable period, then hire an attorney. If it is a case of a major harassment, such as a physical or sexual assault, call an attorney within 24 hours. DO NOT let your school become your sheriff or your attorney! Who has your child's best interests in mind? School administrators often will act to preserve the status quo, and to assume that this, like most disagreements between children, does not pose a real threat. They are not the parents of your child and they do not love your child as you do. Armed with your documented evidence, and your repeated requests for help, you will find that most schools will take responsibility for their actions for fear of someday having to pay for their negligence in court. Court is of course your last resort. But it's there. Ultimately, school districts know this. Sometimes they just need to be reminded.

Looking back, I wished that Jared's school administrators had said two simple words, "We're sorry", and agreed to get Jared some medical and emotional help. That would have been all that was needed to make a young boy feel important and needed by the adults in his school. And it would have helped Jared save face with his fellow students. Instead, the adults who should have cared for him blamed him for his own assault, and the kids in school instinctively knew that the administration would not protect him. They were free to taunt him with comments like, "Ha! I heard you got beat up". ...At least the kids could tell the difference between a fight and an assault!

Step 6 - Help your child to heal
Keep listening and communicating with your child. Ask them questions about how they are doing in school. Some examples might be, "Did you play with anyone on the playground today?" or "Did you sit with anyone at lunch today". You are checking to see if your child is spending any time with friends. A lonely child is at great risk for depression. Keep the communication lines open with your child. Ask your child often about the bullying and whether the situation has improved.

Consider getting your child in to see a counselor or therapist. Check with the school district to see if they have any qualified counselors who have dealt with bullying and the conditions it may cause (depression, anxiety, and post traumatic stress disorders).

Follow up frequently with the school and continue to hold them accountable. They need to be proactive in intervening and keeping a close eye on the bully or bullies' behavior.

Find out whom else in your area has children being bullied or who have dealt with bullying. Find out if you can get a current and accurate perspective from them, as they might be a resource for you or your child. Perhaps they have succeeded in eliminating the problem.

Find healing extracurricular activities for your child. There are Boy Scouts, Girl Scouts, and self-defense classes, volunteer and service organizations in the community, church activities, community events, or athletics. Find out what your child's interests and talents are and encourage your child to develop a hobby to support that interest or talent. They are likely to make friends who share their interests. These friends can be a valuable support network to help your child mature naturally, and even thrive, in spite of bullying.

An extremely positive and proactive approach would be to work with your school district to get a quality anti-bullying program into your local schools. This can be a "healing" activity for the entire family. If you raise enough awareness for the subject, then surely your child cannot be quietly bullied any longer. And working to get something positive accomplished in your school may help take away the anger and isolation that victims of bullying harbor inside. Get creative - bullying decreases when students, parents and child activists show their numbers, demanding positive changes inside their schools.

Step 7 - Stay united as a family
Remember that you are not alone. There are a good number of families who have experienced or are experiencing the same problems. You may need to make some hard decisions about your child's safety. If the school refuses to take the steps necessary to protect your child then you will need to take the necessary action to keep your child safe. The new plan may include removing your child from the school and enrolling him/her in a private school, in an internet school, a different school in your city, even a different school district, home schooling or arranging for a private tutor.

Put this in perspective - If a child were being abused at home, the Social Services would have the duty to protect that child and remove that child from the home. Why is it any different if his peers or anyone else is abusing your child at school? You, as a parent have the duty and the right to remove your child from that school. You must make safety decisions for your child's sake. You never know, you may save your child's life, and you most certainly will save your child's emotional health.

Step 8 – Deciding who is accountable
It is understood that a parent has the primary duty of care for his/her child. We will assume for the sake of this discussion, that anyone and

everyone reading this would willingly, fervently, and tirelessly protect their child from bullying.

Where our schools are concerned, some states have passed anti bullying laws that protect victims. In addition, parents and children have some basic human rights in the absence of a state anti bullying law or a school district policy.

In the Supreme Court's 1989 decision, DeShaney v. Winnebago County Department of Social Services, certain questions about a child's safety are answered. This case concerned a young boy, who suffered permanent injury from a severe beating by his father *after* the local department of social services failed to remove him from his father's custody. Using this case, we learn that because school districts are government entities, they too must follow the same due process as social service agencies. (Under that Due Process Clause)

- Government agencies (including school districts), breach its duty of care if it fails to prevent abuse (bullying). Note: By law, schools must "act in behalf of the parent."
- If a Government agency (which includes a school within a school district), has prior knowledge that there is a risk to the safety of a child (student, or students), the agency, (school), either creates or increases the risk that a child will be exposed to acts of violence, by not acting on that knowledge.
- Government agencies (including school districts) may be found civilly liable for violating the due process rights of victims of private violence (bullying) under the doctrine of state-created danger.

What this case also tells us is that it is NOT the school's first duty to educate. A school's first duty is to protect each student from being harmed just as if they were a parent protecting their own child.

It must be clear to parents, however, that a school can only be held responsible if the school has failed to take reasonable care and reasonable precautions. Just because a student has been bullied doesn't mean a school is automatically responsible for it. Schools cannot be held legally liable for something they had no knowledge of. Again, the key to holding the school accountable is record keeping and persistent notification of the bullying activity. Be sure and follow up on the details of your school's anti bullying program (and the state laws that may apply) and remain diligent in pursuing a course of action on behalf of your child.

Step 9 – Become proactive in obtaining laws, rules, policies and procedures to stop the bullying

Bullying is a severe problem in our country. Unless anti-bullying laws are mandated, schools have, at best, a murky incentive to acknowledge school violence (as we have discussed, if they acknowledge problems, they may affect their own standing, and even their bank account). Relying on schools to take the initiative to, 1) embrace dedicating classroom efforts and disciplinary practices to stamp out bullying, and 2) accept responsibility for the safety of our children, has not happened at most schools. As was the case in our lawsuit, there is confusion amongst the parents, teachers and administrators about what the definition of bullying is or how to deal with it when it occurs.

Recent school shootings and the publicity they have received has surprisingly not motivated schools to get organized either. A law however, usually provides the motivation that schools need to actively, consistently, and effectively deal with this issue.

Many schools may have some form of anti bullying policy that simply isn't being consistently enforced and implemented. Too often, anti bullying curriculum and practices are just suggestions that teachers may use, and are not required material enforced by school administrators. You can change that.

Kids have nowhere to turn, and they know it! They feel it. Right now, many students can only hope that the bullying goes away on its own. Moreover, since the practice of "Zero Tolerance" has penalized kids for physically defending themselves, the victim becomes a victim again. Often kids take the abuse in silence; they see no alternative. This is another reason that an actively managed openly enforced anti bullying program should be installed on school campuses.

For a child who is being bullied, time is of the essence. Inactivity can be very costly. How long can bullied children hold out before adults do something to protect them? Every day a child is bullied is an eternity to them. We worry about terrorists coming into our country and doing us harm, but a victim of bullying walks into their school each day knowing their terrorist could strike any moment and destroy their wounded spirit again, and again. I have heard people say that bullying is a terrible problem for our children. A problem, yes, but a child's problem? I disagree. I say it is an adult problem. As an analogy, that would be like throwing a child that can't swim into a lake and saying, "Hey, you've got a problem!"

Adults are in charge and only adults can set the rules, laws, policies and procedures that will stop bullying.

Step 10 – Work with your School Board

Our federal elected officials are responsible for the safety of all U.S. citizens and our state elected officials are responsible for the safety of the citizens in their state. Likewise, elected school board members are responsible for the safety of their school district citizens, their students and faculty. I challenge all of those who are reading this chapter to go to your school district offices and ask what the written policy is on bullying. If there is no policy, go to a school board meeting and ask the board members to make a policy on bullying. In a day and age of school shootings, assaults, rapes, cyberbashing and numerous other criminal activities, how is it possible that there would not be a school district policy on bullying? Maybe, it's because no one asked the board to get one. Maybe board members did not think it was important enough. Well, it is time to take some action to help curb the epidemic.

As a former school board member myself, I know the importance to act on safety and welfare issues. If, during a meeting, I found that a student's safety was in question because of bullying, I would have a moral responsibility, and a legal obligation, to act. Board members are not beyond being personally sued – the legal question would be, "what did I know, when did I know it, and what action did I take?"

Don't think twice about replacing a board member at the next election cycle if they do not care enough about your child, or any child, to enact an anti bullying policy. They were elected to be sure all children have a safe environment to learn in. If they are not doing their job, vote them out and put someone on the board that will care.

How long can a child play on the freeway dodging cars before the experience finally becomes too much and the child is "hit" and goes over the edge? Will that child hurt another, or will they hurt themselves to solve their pain?

Bullying is a lifetime sentence that victims never forget and some will, or have, never gotten over it. Think for just a moment, do you remember the name or face of your school bully? I'm in my 50's now, but I can still remember the name of the girl who bullied me when I was 15...Debbie.

Looking forward – It is time that every school in America has a clear direction to stop the hurt and pain that goes on every day in a place where our children should feel safe and secure.

Girl to Girl Bullying

"Don't be afraid of the school, the teachers or administrators. You must remember they work for you, and your children. If you don't stand up for your child, who will?"

Corinne's Story
"Just Go Home and Kill Yourself"

In loving memory of Corinne Wilson
09/30/91 – 10/06/04
By Rochelle Sides

As I walked up the stairs to my room, I thought to myself, "She is going to be so excited." I had just bought her a new karaoke machine to practice on. As I approached my room, I saw her feet hanging off the edge of my bed as if she had been waiting for me to come home and had fallen asleep.

I walked up to her, talking to her the entire time. I can't remember exactly what I was saying. I am pretty sure it was something like, "Hey, Corinne wake up, I have a surprise for you."

When I got to where she was, I thought she was playing a joke on me. I thought for a split second that she was wearing a Halloween mask. I shook her and laughed as I was saying, "Good one, Corinne, you got me."

Instantly I realized what I was seeing — what had happened.

I screamed as I started backwards. I screamed so loud I thought my head would explode. I just screamed over and over, as I punched walls and kicked floors. I hit anything that was near me, as if I was trying to fight something — something evil "No, No, No, not my baby, not Corinne, not my Corinne!"

Corinne was special from the day she was born. She had an air about her — a look. You knew she was going to be amazing. She was born Sept. 30, 1991, with piercing blue eyes and soft, blond, curly hair.

She was my youngest, my baby, and my only little girl. I could not believe how incredibly beautiful she was — those eyes, that beautiful hair and her flawless olive skin. She was precious.

She talked very early and once she started, she didn't stop. Corinne could talk to you for hours, and I loved to listen to her. She always had such a loving outlook on life. It seemed as if she was an old soul — wise beyond her years.

She walked early. From then on she ran everywhere, as if she had so much to learn and not enough time to learn it all.

I met my husband, Johnny, who Corinne knew as "Daddy," when she was barely three. We all moved to Texas from Alaska in 1995. Corinne seemed to blossom under all of the love that my husband's family gave her, especially her Grandma Jewel, who fell madly in love with Corinne.

Corinne's first years of school were wonderful. She loved kindergarten and her teacher. She won a spelling bee in the first grade. In second and third grade, she had many friends and academically did very well.

Those were the happiest times in her short life. She woke up every morning wanting to go to school, wanting to see her friends, and most importantly feeling good about herself.

Everything changed when we moved to Rockdale, Texas in 2000.

Corinne had trouble from the first day. She missed her old school and friends and didn't feel as if she fit in there.

I signed her up to play softball to help her meet people. Unfortunately, this made the situation worse. Corinne's shyness was mistaken for conceit, and she was placed on a team with more experienced girls. They teased her relentlessly about her inability. She would cry after every practice.

She did not want me to say anything to anyone, afraid that would make the bullying worse. But I finally had enough. I spoke to the coach about the teasing and it stopped, but now the girls would have nothing to do with Corinne.

I felt helpless. I wanted her to be involved, and I wanted her to have friends. I wanted the old Corinne back. She was no longer excited; she no longer wanted to go to school.

I told her to be nice to one person everyday and soon she would have a friend. It worked. She had a friend, she was so happy. For the next year and a half, things appeared to go smoothly. We felt as if we had made it over the hump. Corinne finished the fifth grade and was so excited about going to middle school. She was now entering the sixth grade, excelling in academics and becoming a beautiful young woman.

I felt as if I could see parts of the old Corinne again.

I was so excited about the years to come, watching her grow into a woman. I was so very proud of Corinne; she was not only my daughter but also my friend. She and I spent many hours together watching TV, singing our favorite songs, shopping and cooking — all the things that a mother and daughter do together.

As I expected, boys were starting to become interested in her and vice a versa. Why wouldn't they, I knew she was the most beautiful girl I had ever seen.

That is when jealousy reared its ugly head and the bullying began in full force. It was such a confusing time for Corinne. She had no idea why the other girls were mad at her — all she wanted was to be their friend.

They began by excluding her from the group, they would make her cry, and then they would make up. They would tell Corinne she was fat and her hair was frizzy and make fun of her one day, then befriend her the next day.

Corinne was hurt, yet she didn't show it. Instead, as we learned later, she wrote in her journal. She wrote of the pain and confusion, the desperate need to make them like her, the anger at being put in that position, the injustice of it all. She knew she didn't cause it, but she was determined to make it better. She did anything that they wanted her to do in an attempt to get back in their graces.

I knew as the 6th grade wound down that Corinne was on again off again with these girls, but I had no clue of the magnitude of the isolation and confusion my daughter felt. Now, this is something I struggle with daily. My precious, sweet baby did not deserve this. Corinne lived by the rule "Do unto others." She did not understand that they didn't care and they never would.

Over the summer before her 7th grade year, Corinne attended a basketball camp at Baylor University. I was scared and worried, but she was so happy. She ate, slept, and breathed basketball; this was a dream come true for her. When she got home from the camp, she was more confident than I had seen her in a long time. But Corinne's confidence only made the other girls' jealousy increase.

Corinne wrote in her journal everyday about a new hurtful taunt — the lonely, silent treatments and the vicious remarks. "Corinne you are so ugly, you make me want to run into a brick wall." "Corinne your hair is frizzy and you are so fat." "Corinne, you know you can't sing."

Shortly after they really started harassing her, Corinne was selected from more than 500 contestants to sing in a karaoke contest in Waco, at the Heart of Texas Fair and Rodeo. Corinne was happy and proud of herself. And I could not have been happier for her. I knew that she was talented, and I told her all the time how well she sang. Now she had validation.

With each new success Corinne had, the bullies increased the exclusion and harassment. She felt as if she couldn't win. She wanted to sing and she wanted do well in school, but she also wanted friends.

The Theme of the Day
The bullying came to a head on Oct. 6, 2004. That morning in PE, one of the girls slapped her and called her a "whore." Then the girls wrote her notes throughout the day telling her she was fat, ugly and had ratty hair. They said they wished she were dead and that she should "go home and kill herself." These girls decided that this was the "Theme of the Day," that Corinne should go home and kill herself. They recruited other children to tell Corinne to go home and kill herself as well.

Corinne was a very loving and sensitive person. I can only imagine the hurt and confusion my daughter felt that day. These girls were supposed to be her best friends and they wanted her dead. At one point Corinne wrote on her desk in one of her classes, "This school hates me," over and over again. Later I was told that Corinne had her head down and cried most of the day. As Corinne left school that day, these girls said these words one last time, "Go home and kill yourself!"

"Corinne, Corinne, I have a surprise for you" I called as I came home. As I walked upstairs, I had no clue that I was walking into my own personal hell — that I would never be the same, that my life as I knew it, was over, that I would have to live the rest of my life without my baby girl.

The day my husband and I should have been listening to our daughter perform at the rodeo, cheering her on; full of pride and love, we buried her instead. We buried her dreams, her future and her promise.

After Corinne's death, my husband and I requested meetings with the principal of her school. We needed to know what happened that day. What had gone wrong? We met with more than resistance; it was complete denial and outright lies about the events of that day. The administrators expected us to believe that not one child had told them about what had happened the day Corinne died.

The principal refused us access to Corinne's teachers. According to him, they were too upset to talk to us. More upset than we were? Her parents? We raised her. We loved her more than life itself. If they were upset, perhaps it was because they had not done anything to prevent the tragic consequences of Corinne's last day of torment inside their school.

At the second meeting, we were told that this would be the last meeting concerning this matter, as if the death of our daughter was no longer their problem. We were furious! We went to the police. There we were met with the same lack of concern and trivialization. We were actually told it was "kids being kids."

For me that was the last straw. It was as if Corinne did not matter. The pain of losing our daughter is unquantifiable; there are no words to describe the loneliness and despair that we have experienced over the last two years and continue to struggle with everyday.

I refused to let them off that easy. I started to search. I knew there had to be a law against what happened to my little girl. I first went to the school district website and did a search on the word "bullying." I found nothing, not even a mention of the word. My search then expanded to the State of Texas. Again, there was no law against what happened to my daughter. I still find that hard to believe.

What I did find was the Bully Police USA website. I emailed the director, Brenda High, and told her what happened to Corinne, she called me immediately and we spoke for what seemed like hours.

That phone call changed my life.

After talking to Brenda, I knew that I had to speak out about what had happened to Corinne. I spoke to the Senate Education Committee, to State Representatives and to every reporter that would listen. We got their attention. In 2005, Bully Police USA and I were successful in getting an anti-bullying law passed in Texas.

But the law wasn't good enough, so, in 2007, Corinne's Law was introduced before the Texas House and Senate. Bully Police USA graded this possible law an A+, but unfortunately, it failed to pass in the last days of the session. However, with the help of Bully Police USA, we will continue to work hard to get this law passed in the next session...for all children that attend school in Texas.

I will continue this fight for Corinne and all the other children that are being bullied for as long as necessary. We as adults must stand together and protect our children against an old system of denial and cover up. They ALL deserve as much.

Relational Aggression
Girl-to-Girl Bullying Examined
By Corinne's mom, Rochelle Sides

What is "Relational Aggression"?
The encyclopedia defines relational aggression as psychological (social/emotional) <u>aggression</u> between people in relationships. Psychologists describe it as a behavior designed to manipulate relationships in order to hurt a particular individual.

However, relational aggression is much more complicated than that.

Today we now know that relational aggression is a tool used by many young girls and women to improve social status, exert power, camouflage insecurities or act on jealousies. It is directed at intended victims using any number of methods: rumors, lies, secrets, insults, exclusion, violence, to elevate their social standing in a group or groups. These actions can also be identified as bullying, female aggression or social aggression. Due to its covert and secretive nature, it is rarely done in the presence of adults, and it is hard to detect, control and prevent.

Effects of Relational Aggression – Short and Long Term
Research has shown that the common short-term effects of relational aggression are embarrassment, confusion, anger, fear, humiliation, loneliness, betrayal, self-consciousness and sadness. On the more serious side, the long-term effects of relational aggression can be depression, lower grades, drug and alcohol use, low self worth, eating disorders, thoughts of suicide, suicide attempts and... completion. National data reports say that children are most concerned and hurt by emotional violence. A study done by Illinois Wesleyan University shows that relational aggression, in America, affects 1 in every 20 boys — and 1 in every 4 girls. One in four!

Personal Stories of Relational Aggression
The following stories illustrate the pain and power of relational aggression. We offer these as the intimate thoughts of victims of relentless relational aggression; insight into the effects it has, short and long term.

Elizabeth Bennett's Story - Peer Abuse
"When I was growing up, my first memory of being bullied occurred at around the age of three. I was outside on my carport and I remember two older children from the neighborhood come over and started throwing rocks at me. As I grew into elementary

school, it continued. I was in three different schools during that period and remember being blamed for things the bullies would do. I would get my head slapped, I'd be pushed, my hair pulled, I was spit at, and had my clothes hidden and thrown around before and after gym class. It was hard to focus in school as a result of these things. When I moved in the 4th grade, I encountered my first "Queen Bee" and could never understand why everyone felt she was so wonderful. I found her to be quite rude and snippy; at least she was with me.

"In middle school, my reputation hit the rumor mill. I remember going to school and having people laugh and point at me; to this day, I do not know what those rumors were. I just know that the Queen Bee was behind them. I also found out later that her mother helped to fuel them with other adults. School, church, anywhere I went, there they were.

"In the 8th grade, I remember coming home from school one day and dealing with the usual spitting in the hair, pulling of hair and its varieties. However, they added a new twist that day. The bullies decided to put green slime in my hair. The kind that came from the green toy garbage pail that was so popular during the late 70's and early 80's. I went home and washed that stuff out of my hair and just cried. Why couldn't this stop? It was also during this period that I encountered my first bout with clinical depression. At 12, I almost attempted bullycide. A good day for me was going to school and not having anyone bother me.

"By the time I entered high school, I was vulnerable, incredibly insecure and tried to the point of absurdity to get to know people. All I wanted was friends, but again, this left me a target. The bullying and psychological effects were too overwhelming. I was depressed, fearful and wanted to just vanish. They wanted to "kick my butt" for things I never even did. They'd just hassle me in the halls, in class and anywhere else. I started to sneak alcohol and failed the 9th grade. I was moved to another school to repeat the 9th grade. Of course, more bullying and relational aggression continued there. I went through high school in a daze, drinking, smoking and even doing some drugs. I let people take advantage of me and destroy me and my property. I could not even think clearly and when I think back to those days, I still cannot think or see them clearly. I just know I was depressed, having nightmares regularly, hated school and hated my life. I attempted bullycide at 17 and tried again at 18. I just wanted the depression and PTSD to go away.

"I went to teachers and my parents even went to teachers and administrators during these years but nobody would help or even listen. Nobody. My parents were frustrated, and it never ended. I was told I was "too sensitive" or this was "all in my head" and if I "changed this or that" then it would stop. Of course, it never stopped. One Administrator even got involved, going so far as to tell me that I would be lucky if I got a job working in a grocery store and to forget college all together. Well, I now have a Masters Degree so I proved them wrong, huh?

"In college, I found another way to cope away from alcohol and drugs. I become a compulsive studier and it worked! It kept me away from having to be around people yet it fueled my depression and isolation; the issues were still there. I started getting really angry about all of this, started putting up walls and holding grudges. I started to develop social anxiety along with the depression. I graduated college with a 3.1 grade point average, but was depressed and socially anxious. Welcome to adulthood!

"At the age of 24, I was diagnosed with clinical depression. I still felt isolated and alone and scared of people. At this point, I was terrified of my peer group and did not want anything to do with them. As I entered the workforce, I encountered bullying twice in my first job. It threw me off and kept me off kilter. I had a terrible time concentrating. In the second job, I refused to be bullied and did all I could to prevent that from happening. Confronting the bully made it much worse. My job became trying to not be the target and trying so hard to please others, rather than my assigned responsibilities. At the age of 31, I had enough. I had a nervous breakdown and just could not take it anymore.

"It has been a few years since my nervous breakdown. I have slowly built myself up again after reaching that very low point. I consider myself a survivor, although it would be more accurate to say "I'm surviving". The past trauma of bullying still affects me; it is very hard to be out in a group of people, mainly in odd numbers. I will not work in an environment unless it is a pleasant environment with no bullying. I battle clinical depression as well. I am afraid of getting too close to others; trust is incredibly hard for me. I am not married as I still have issues with intimacy. I am on medication for these problems. I am in therapy. I do not stop though. I keep going and working towards healing and relearning healthy attitudes and behaviors. I now know I am not the terrible person I was led to believe I was all of those years. I refuse to be bullied. I actually like myself now and feel I am okay. I am learning to let the walls down when I sense I can trust someone. I know my triggers and avoid the situations that can encourage them. I have my life and all of this 'illness' and the scars from being bullied do not control me anymore. I do what works for me, one day at a time. I think that is all anyone can do."

More Stories of Relational Aggression

Tiffani's Story—15 years old

"For the past three years I have gotten bullied a lot. The school has done nothing to stop it. They have had meetings with the kids that are doing the bullying and of course while they have the kids there they say "oh we will stop" but that's when it gets worse. I started high school this year. And it seems to have gotten even worse. I'm getting picked on every single day. I have missed so much school because I have stress, depression, anxiety and all that kind of stuff. The school seems not to realize that the bullying is just adding more stress on me and is ending my chances of getting an education. I can't *take much more of this ... I can't take much more of anything. I told my school. They said I have emotional problems and I have to deal with them. They say to just forget everything that is happening to me. Well I can't anymore. I'm at the point I cry myself to sleep at night. I'm scared to walk alone in the hallways of school. And I'm cutting myself because of the pain. I don't want to deal with the pain. Please help me!"*

High School Girl

"Every morning I wake up and ask why am I still here? I hate it (bullying). I wish I could be dead, the way some people talk to me and act towards me. It's continuous, it never stops. Every day I get up and go to school knowing what will happen and it hurts to think about it. I can tell my dad or mom what happens at school but every time I do they say you need to learn how to get along with others. They don't know what it is like for me. I have not tried suicide but I think that if these kids do not stop I will. Instead of suicide I cut myself. I would like to be set on fire and burn, then have to go back to a place where kids pick on me. I get hit in the halls and everyone will turn and laugh. One time I had a crush on a popular kid and his girlfriend would write notes saying they were from him. They were cruel notes. It hurts to know no one likes me."

High School Girl

"I have always been bullied by my peers, both girls and boys, through verbal abuse, physical abuse, mental abuse, in every way they could think of. I am now in the 10th grade and throughout the years of my life have changed schools four times, all for the same reason; I was being bullied. I never fit in with any group. I was always an outsider looking in. No one wants to believe that they are the ones being laughed at, but I am. The popular girls used to make fun of me for my hair; they used to say that I was stupid, or laugh at me."

High School Girl

"When I was in elementary school, I was teased a lot. Different people called me names like fatso, ugly, and would talk about me when they thought I wasn't listening. I couldn't begin to tell you what they would do when the teachers were not around. One thing I will not forget is how they would push me and throw things at my head. At night I would go into my room and shut the door. I would stay up crying and wishing I were dead. I have tried to kill myself many times. Now I am in high school and nothing has changed. I still want to die, but I go to counseling to get help. I wish something could be done to stop this."

Things You Should Know About Female Bullying

- Female bullying is different from male bullying. Many times girls do not fit exclusively into one category -- bully, victim or bystander.
- Very often, their behavior depends on the situation. They may

alternate roles depending on who they are with and the dynamics of the current social structure.

- Girls are known to be less physical and more "discreet" in their bullying than boys. This may be because girls are socialized to avoid overt and physical displays of anger. In order to express their feelings, they resort to subversive and passive-aggressive forms of interaction which are less visible to adults.
- It is important to "keep tabs" on girls, even if you (or they) do not think they are being bullied, because they themselves may often not realize what is going on. If a girl tells her she's "fat," that's bullying. Such comments are often internalized, and never forgotten. If she's not included in a sleepover, she may believe she doesn't deserve to go. These comments and power plays can be internalized until her self-concept and self-esteem are slowly destroyed; all without her knowing what is happening or before any adult can intervene.
- The slow degradation of self esteem induced by chronic bullying is difficult to appreciate. It is important to be ever-vigilant for early warning signs, to catch the problem before it is too late.

Helping the Victim

Encourage communication – get the girl to talk. Talking to a trusted caring person reduces the isolation of a victim and helps build-up her confidence so she can face the problem. This may be the one thing that best prevents a girl from going to an extreme (such as suicide) to cope with the situation.

Be an ally. Any girl who is being victimized by bullying and aggression needs to know she can enlist the help and support of adults if necessary. In many cases the problem has become "too big" for her to handle alone. Telling a child or group of children to "just work it out" is not helpful. Remember that female aggression is more difficult to pinpoint and prove, so intervening in these situations may not be "cut and dry." Each situation is different.

Changing behaviors that teach new skills. Girls can learn better ways for coping with victimization, which may include:

- Standing up to the bully verbally
- Using humor
- Walking away
- Changing behaviors and patterns that create a larger target for bullies. (instead of that provoke the bullying)
- Building friendships with others that can be a support system

We should call special attention to a skill that relates to all of the above. Probably the most important skill that can be taught to girls is how to be assertive and straightforward in their expression of frustration and anger. Developing a strong sense of self is the key to avoiding the victim mentality and makes a girl more likely to deal with bullies effectively.

Foster self-esteem. Help the girl find ways to feel successful in other areas of her life such as academics, hobbies, interests, athletics, etc. When she has a strong base within herself, she is better able to face social difficulties.

Helping the Bystander

Other children are always aware of bullying incidents at school and elsewhere. They should be made aware of the dangers of bullying and taught to intervene when it's safe, or report bullying incidents when they see it. Adults need to be aware that bullying is a very common problem that is often kept hidden from their view. They should be always vigilant for the signs and behaviors. No one should stand by idly and let bullying continue.

Send the message. All kids and parents in a community should be aligned in anti bullying efforts. Bullying should never be tolerated. Kids should be held accountable for how they treat each other in effective, consistent, ways whether the setting is home, school, community groups/clubs, sports teams, etc. Sending clear messages of the ramifications of bullying behavior is a strong aid in limiting its popularity.

Teach peaceful intervention. Adults can help kids learn how to recognize unsafe and abusive relational patterns, and how to intervene peacefully. Instilling a "do the right thing" group mentality in children, advocating intervention when appropriate, is another way to reduce the isolation of a victim, and eradicate bullying. Adults should be committed to taking reports of relational aggression seriously and assisting when necessary. Please see the list of resources in the back of this book for more information on this topic.

Not helping is hurting. Teach student-group strategies that support the victim and make sure that bystanders know the proper channels for getting someone the help they need.

Watching while someone is abused or bullied is unacceptable. If a child is uncomfortable intervening, then they need to feel comfortable sharing information with the appropriate adult figure. Inaction simply emboldens the bullies.

Helping the Bully
Certainly it is not doing a child bully any good to allow such behavior to continue. We are not creating productive future members of our societies if we allow bullies to get away with their actions. Adult intervention is critical in this effort.

Let her know, that you know. Bullies who use relational and passive aggression to inflict pain on others believe that their behavior flies "under the radar" with adults. Unfortunately, this is often the case. As an adult, once you have detected the pattern, it is helpful to call out the behavior. Even if the girl denies it, she knows that you are aware of her tactics and may think twice before bullying again.

Teach acceptable ways of expressing anger. Girls tend to use relational and passive aggression because it has been more socially acceptable than physical aggression. If girls are going to stop the passive aggression, they need to learn new methods for coping with and expressing anger. Once girls find success with these better methods, they are more likely to reduce the abusive patterns. Again, please see the list of resources at the back of this book for useful methods to instill changes in this behavior.

Hold subversive bullies accountable. Relational aggression can literally ruin a girl's self-esteem and positive outlook on life. It is a form of harassment -- NOT freedom of speech, as some believe. As previously mentioned, these epidemic behaviors will decrease only when the aggressors are held accountable

Tips for Educators
Educators and teachers can have a profound effect on reducing bullying behavior. Recent efforts in schools are focusing on a peer to peer regulated environment that sanctions against, rather than ignores or condones, the kinds of continuing hurtful actions that occur in bully/victim relationships. Empowering and encouraging children and teenagers to be 'everyday policeman' of their own environments, combined with awareness at the familial level, has proven very effective in controlling and reducing bullying. The most successful interventions take place simultaneously at the individual, dyad, peer, classroom, school and family levels.

Suggestions for teachers and administrators
- Schedule a full staff meeting to raise awareness and knowledge
- Find out what other schools have done

- Find out existing programs or initiatives in your school, district, or state – **Develop an anti-bullying policy.**
- Consult with teachers, students, parents and other school personnel
- Incorporate anti-bullying education with curriculum work and existing policies
- Improve playground and hall security and monitoring
- Implement peer support services such as peer counseling
- Increase adult supervision at key times (lunch, recess, etc.)

My daughter Corinne was a classic victim of relational aggression. It started slowly with rumors, secrets and exclusion; it progressed to harassment and violence. Like most victims of relational aggression, Corinne blamed herself for her bully's behavior. She internalized her pain and kept the bullying to herself in an attempt to maintain a relationship with her bullies, as many girls do. As a result, it damaged her self-esteem and caused severe depression, which ultimately led to Corinne taking her life.

Relational aggression interferes with an adolescent's sense of self. Insecurity may persist throughout adult life. As described in one of the above stories, even if a child endures and survives bullying, the ability to trust others and the ability to have healthy and supportive adult relationships is diminished if not destroyed. Girl to girl relational bullying develops unhealthy patterns for handling adverse emotions and circumstances, and no one is immune to its effects...victims, bystanders, or bullies.

Hazing:
Another Form of Bullying

"Don't be fooled. Bullying doesn't have to be repeated, or take place over a period of time. Each child is different. Even one traumatic instance can cripple a young mind into a well of despair."

Matt's Story
"Rite of Passage"

In loving memory of Matthew Alexander Epling – 2/10/88 – 7/16/02
By Tammy Epling

We brought our first-born child home on Valentine's Day 1988, a fitting gift that we would cherish for a lifetime. As I held my precious newborn tenderly in my arms, he took my breath away. I never knew that you could love someone so deeply. I was amazed how this love came so easily, a love like no other - a love so strong, so unconditional, so protective; It was natural. Little did I know that in 14 years, 5 months, 6 days, 1 hour and 19 minutes, a silent killer I knew nothing about would tear him from my arms.

How could this happen? I was always such an attentive mom, so diligent when it came to my child. I never missed a soccer game or Boy Scout meeting. I got a subscription to Parents Magazine and studiously read each issue from cover to cover. I made sure I took him to swimming lessons, so he would never drown. I taught him about strangers, so he would never be kidnapped. It may sound corny but I even taught him never to stand by a tree in a lightning storm. However, it never occurred to me to tell him that words and mean actions can hurt or possibly kill.

Matt was born with a strong personality — he was always on the go. He walked at nine months of age and he was talking by the time he was a year. One of his first words was "Batman." He loved superheroes and Ninja Turtles. Matt taught himself to ride a two-wheeler at the age of four, and he jumped his first curb at five (one of many). He switched between skateboards, roller blades and bikes, and dreamt of becoming a pro-skater or pro-biker. He was great at math and might have become an engineer if the Tony Hawk thing did not pan out. One thing for sure, if it was a nice day, you could always find Matt in front of our house, practicing stunts on a ramp that he and his dad built.

Matt always liked to stand out in the crowd. In the eighth grade, Matt decided to grow out his hair - that thick wavy hair. He told me the "bedhead look" was in, he was getting it started, and by next fall, it would be the new fad. Do not be fooled though, he worked hard to make sure that his hair was just right. If when he woke up and it was too "poofy", he would sit at the table with his bike helmet on, eating his cereal, until his hair flattened to the perfect style. Today I laugh when I see the "bedhead" look at the malls, and I think of Matt.

Matt also discovered theater that year. In May of 2002, he did an excerpt from Huckleberry Finn. He was supposed to perform with two other students, but they did not show, so he went on solo. He was awesome. I sat hanging on his every word. I was stunned and in awe. Who knew? Afterward a woman came up to Matt so she could see if his accent was real or not.

What Matt really loved was comedy improv. He was quick and witty and loved to show off. Matt spent hours taping "Whose Line is it Anyway?" for his teacher to review. His teacher credits him for giving her the vision to create such a class. It is now a popular class at the middle school. This past spring, we were honored by a performance from the current class, a tribute to Matt from his teacher. Tears mingled with laughter as we watched the students perform. Matt would have loved the attention.

Matt loved all areas of art. He was just learning to play the guitar. He also enjoyed drawing, or doodling as he called it. In all sense of the word, he was an artist. He and some friends painted a comic mural of a giraffe affectionately referred to as Girrafo. It adorned the cafeteria wall until the school was remodeled.

Matt could also write. For such a cool exterior, he still had a sensitive side. In his "Window" poem, for which he won an award, he found beauty in his own back yard. Through poetry, he could find magic in a snowfall, his grandfather's mementos or even a simple tree. His poem, "The Willow", was read at his class' commencement ceremony:

I know the willow
I know the willow with its strong branches protruding out of the trunk
I know the willow with its roots growing deep, deep in the earth.
To the very center.

My soul is the willow
My soul grows with the willow, growing stronger and older.
As the willow takes the air and water in, I too take in. I take in things I like and I hold
them close and others, the ones that may hurt me I shield.

I know the willow
The willow is beautiful and so is my soul and I am beautiful.
Me and the willow are the same, but we are different.
We are both unique but then the willow is only a tree and I am only me.
But neither I, nor the willow, can be changed in our ways

Matt was a typical teenager in every sense. Yes, he could be moody and demanding, but that glowing smile came back every time. He had an opinion on everything, and he was certain he was always right. He could become upset when the rain spoiled his plans. Matt saw himself as a winner, an achiever, never wanting to lose at anything. He could be a sore loser. Matt was an active learner, always absorbing information. Sometimes he did not like being serious and would often crack a joke when things got too heavy.

Life with Matt was never dull; he had all kinds of ideas. Once, he got upset when he was too small to fit into the clothes at the skateboard shop. He was determined that he would start a ME (for both "me" and Matt Epling) collection of smaller frame clothes for skate boarders. He was always so noisy...even when he was reading; his empty hand would be drumming out a steady beat with the end of his pencil.

On June 7, 2002, Matt left the eighth grade, content, happy and proud of his accomplishments. He had been voted in the mock elections as the guy with the best smile, the best personality, funniest guy and the kid most likely to be an actor. Who knew, that on the last day of school, all he worked so hard for would be stripped away from him in a single act of humiliation? That day Matt was at home with a friend playing video games when a knock at the door interrupted them. Some other friends wanted Matt to go on a bike ride...

Little did Matt know that lurking around the corner was a parked car, and three upperclassmen waiting for him.

The upperclassmen restrained Matt and his friend and said, "Welcome to high school". Then they proceeded to pour syrup on them, and smash eggs on their heads. Matt fought back and stood up for himself and his friend. The main attacker, who outweighed Matt by 50 pounds and towered a full foot taller than Matt, was angered even more. It became even more violent, until one of the other older boys stepped in to stop it. The main attacker told Matt "Stop fighting. This is how it is!"

My son called my husband at work, upset and humiliated. He arrived less than five minutes after the attack. After being sure that Matt was not physically harmed, he called the police. When I arrived home, the police were still there, and I saw Matt and his friend still dripping with eggs. Matt was very upset that his favorite skateboard shoes were now ruined. The police said it was an assault and battery and a report was taken. (Later we would find out that the police went back to the precinct and spent all of 20 minutes on this before their shift ended. We did not hear back from them about the incident for at least three weeks.)

Was this "hazing" somehow to be expected for incoming ninth graders? How can a civilized city allow such a thing? Afterwards, a neighbor told me that this had been a long-standing "tradition," and the schools and police simply looked the other way. Another neighbor noted that the people involved had prior issues with the school.

We talked to Matt about the incident and, for the most part, he seemed okay. He wanted them to do some type of community service for their actions. My husband called the police every day the week after the incident and left messages. He was leaving for a business trip to China, and we wanted some resolution before he left. The police did not return any of his calls. My husband even took a call from one of the boy's parents who were upset that we had called the police and now "their" child was going to get in trouble because of "us" calling the police.

I think what hurt Matt the most was that people he considered friends had lured him from our house and placed him into this situation. (Later we found out that these friends were threatened to take part in the ordeal or face the consequences)

We knew the attackers were aware that the police had been called, but that nothing had been done. Looking back, I felt this left plenty of opportunity, even motive, for possible retribution. I had a long talk with Matt while his father was away. He said there were things he did not want to tell the police, but should have, because he was embarrassed. He mentioned that the hood was up on the car, because they hid behind it and the engine was running. Matt was afraid that he might get pushed into the engine during the scuffle. Matt also said that the attackers used obscenities during the assault, and that the main aggressor had threatened to kill him if he told anyone.

Matt seemed to be dealing with this situation fine and we had no immediate worries. He went on to get a part-time job at a local supermarket, for which he was very proud. He knew what he was going to do with his first check — he had gone online and researched several companies to find the perfect BMX bike. I went with him and purchased the $400 bike on his behalf. He agreed to pay a little from each check until it was paid off. Finally, the police called. They set a date to meet with us to talk about the case and that the investigation would begin. This was set for July 17, a full month and a half from the June 7th incident.

July 16 was a perfect day in the heart of summertime. It was normal day in every way. I knocked on Matt's door to wake him so I could go over the day's agenda with him before I headed off to work. Matt was usually grumpy in the mornings as he had grown accustomed to sleeping until noon. So, I sent in his best friend, Lewis, his dog, to wake him. As grumpy as he might be, he usually could not resist a smile when Lewis woke him. Today was no exception.

Matt was proud of the fact that he was only fourteen and had landed a job. I worried if it would be too much pressure and responsibility for him. I remember when I took him for his first day of work; I could not leave the store. I just lingered there. I wanted to make sure he was okay. It was that same nervous feeling I felt when I stood outside his kindergarten door the first day of school.

Matt seemed to like his job, and it gave him something to do in the summer. He was so active that I worried about him getting bored. I reminded him that I would call him around 2 p.m. to make sure he was ready for work. He planned to ride his bike. Then I would pick him up at 7 p.m., after work. When I called that afternoon, he sounded a bit quiet, perhaps still tired. I came home from work and took my daughter and her friend to the water park up the road. When we got home, Matt called to tell me not to pick him up. His friend had stopped by the store, and they were going to go to his house. He sounded upbeat and excited about this change in plans; he might even spend the night. I took advantage of the situation.

I left my daughter and her friend with my husband and went in search of the perfect book for my book club to read. I stayed at the bookstore a bit longer than I intended, a decision that would relentlessly haunt me. As I drove back into my neighborhood, I heard sirens. This was not unusual, as the fire station is literally at the end of our street. If it wasn't for all the trees, you could probably see it from our roof. I quickly pulled over; I could not get very close to my house. My first thought was that there was a fire, but I didn't see any smoke. A neighbor told me they were all at my house. My house?! At first, I thought maybe Matt had put the popcorn in the microwave for too long again. It's probably something like that.

My neighbor held my hand and we walked in together. I was still in denial that anything serious could have happened. When I walked in, I squinted, as I was blinded by all the patterns on the wall by the flashing lights. There were men inside — firefighters, police officers. No one said anything to me at first, and then a man said my son was upstairs. My husband came down with an empty blank look and told me Matt was messing around, and had twisted a belt around his neck. He said it so matter of fact, as if it was no different than when Matt had broken the garage window with his basketball. I just knew it still was not serious. Surely, they had reached him in time, and any minute Matt would come downstairs.

I do not know how much time passed, everything seemed like slow motion. I then heard the hysterical screams of my daughter, "Why did he do that!? Why did he do that!?" That is when I froze in terror. This must be serious! Then they brought Matt down the stairs. He looked so pale. I did not know that he was barely clinging to life. There was only room for one parent in the ambulance, so my husband would go, and a neighbor would drive me.

The 10-minute trip to the hospital took forever. I felt a panic like no other. It's like that feeling every parent has when you lose sight of your child in a crowded mall. It was like that intense panic that takes over, then you find them, and you relax. Now I was stuck in that horrific panic state. I could not stand it a moment longer. I screamed to God to please let him be okay! I prayed. I screamed. I begged. I bargained. Please, I'll do anything; just do not take my son!

When we arrived at the emergency room, I ran in. I barely had time to enter the door when a person quickly whisked me into a small room. My husband held me as he told me Matt was gone. I cried, as I pounded his chest, NO, NO, NO. I screamed inside. Every sound was muffled like I was underwater. Teary-eyed family members with concerned looks on their faces surrounded me, but I felt helpless and alone. Wake me up! I thought I must have fallen asleep. Please! Someone! Wake me up from this horrible nightmare.

Things seemed real but they could not be. When we needed to say goodbye, I did not want to view Matt's body because that made it real. I resisted as long as I could. This was not a "body"; this was my boy, my son. Finally, I had to do it. I reluctantly walked down the hallway to the room where my son lay. As I stood in the doorway, I felt a hand in the small of my back gently push me in. I heard someone say that sometimes their souls stay for a while to hear their goodbyes. I entered the room, I wanted to say something profound, but all I could utter in a hoarse whisper was, "I love you, Matt."

The funeral was like watching a slow motion movie that I was actually appearing in. I felt like I was behind a sheet of glass watching it unfold. Nothing seemed real. The days that followed Matt's death was unbearable. Time seemed to stand still and minutes dragged on like hours. It was impossible to accomplish the smallest task. Our once-noisy bustling house with kids running in and out was quiet. When Matt died, they stopped coming, and so did his sister's friends. Our daughter would say the house just is not fun anymore without Matt. When Matt was on his ramp, we often had kids in front of our house watching. Now our neighbors laid flowers and notes on Matt's ramp for us to show they cared, and that they too grieved our loss. Still, our house was somber and silent.

Summer came to an end and school started. Matt would have been a freshman. We contacted the school and asked what was going to be done to help the students and how we could help? How was this tragedy to be handled and what about Matt's friends? We were very concerned for them. We met with the then-superintendent and asked questions, including what action was being taken against the returning student who assaulted Matt? He said they would handle it and would contact us and let us know what was happening. We were never contacted by the school, and to this day we have never received an answer to that nagging question.

Shortly after school started, a friend of Matt's stopped by and told us about high school - what he was doing, what it was like, and yes he said they observed a moment silence for Matt one morning; a moment of silence to recap a lifetime of moments. That night I cried myself to sleep, as I had never cried before; a deep wailing sound came from me deep inside my soul. I cried this time, not only because I missed Matt, but for all he was missing. Perhaps, in those split seconds he could not see what others saw in him and what he meant to so many.

None of this made sense. There was little I could find relief in: I was restless, trapped in my thoughts. I knew people who lost children, but not to suicide. I had to put the pieces together; I had to know why this happened. I kept going back to the hazing; it was the only thing out of the ordinary. At the time of Matt's death, we did not immediately link the two incidents, but we were not trained to. That was someone else's job.

Now, thinking back about the period after the hazing, Matt seemed a bit quieter and a bit more compliant, which was unusual for him. I thought with his job that perhaps he was maturing and did not think too much of the incident. I did notice he was more argumentative with his sister, and at times, really mean. Was that a sign? I got down on him instead of asking him why he was doing it. Were all these very subtle signs? Was he actually depressed about the situation? Yes, in hindsight he probably was. I have read that those who are bullied or hazed tend to take out their anger on others. As siblings, he and his sister had always argued from time to time, but this was something more.

It would be a while before the death investigation was closed. I thought that surely one of Matt's friends might know what he was thinking. Did he tell a friend he was depressed? Did someone else see a difference in Matt? Often kids will tell a friend rather than a parent. There would have to be some information from somewhere. Surely, I would gain some insight into why. What hurt Matt so intensely that he would contemplate such harm to himself?

I would literally sit paralyzed on my couch, my mind racing, going over every single detail of that summer. I went over the parts he did not confess to the police: How they told him they would kill my son if he told, how they threatened him. How scared Matt must have been, although he tried not to show it. I hoped the police might find something out when they investigated Matt's last day. Were his attackers in the store that day? Did they make one last threat or even a mean gesture? Had they been bothering him after the assault? They have cameras at the store; maybe they captured something. The police would ask these questions, right? I went back over his entire life repeatedly, looking for clues. Matt's personality really had not changed. He had never hurt himself; he had just bought his new bike and had $200 dollars in his wallet. Every avenue I went down I ended up at the same place where I started, the day of the hazing.

In October a detective left a message on Kevin's work phone that Matt's death was ruled a suicide. It was an impersonal way to find out the outcome of their investigation. Later we finally got a copy of the death investigation to review. I was outraged at what I read. Aside from us, only two of Matt's friends were questioned. The school was not contacted about any behavior issues; Matt's doctor was not even contacted. As we read on, we found that no one even went to the store to see if anything happened while Matt was working. The main thrust of the questioning of Matt's friends was about the hazing incident, and how angry Matt had felt.

A case-review letter from the prosecutor noted that; "(Matt) was angry and sullen at times and had to be disciplined from time to time". Those words were like acid on my heart. Another piece of Matt stripped away. Yes, he was angry, angry about being hazed, as it was the main point of police questioning to his friends. In addition, there was no mention of excessive discipline anywhere in the report. Only Kevin's reference that, yes, he was disciplined when he was younger. So, if we had said we never disciplined him, would that have been used against us, too? How could the questioning be about us and not about the hazing? Why wasn't that looked at as a contributing factor?

Don't we, as a society, have moral obligations to protect our most precious possessions? Every child assaulted deserves a thorough investigation. If Matt had died another way, in a car or a bike accident, they would have investigated it fully, right? To us, it seemed like it was easier for the police to put Matt's death into the suicide category than to spend the extra time asking a few more questions.

Suicide is now the number three killer of our young people and the children that are dying are getting younger every year. One would think law enforcement would try to gather every bit of information possible. In our search for answers, we took part in a study from a local university. We completed a post-mortem personality evaluation on Matt to see if perhaps we missed something. My husband and I answered close to 250 detailed questions about Matt, first separately then together. The findings were relatively normal. Matt ranked 10 percent over normal in the area of being defensive, and I remember it saying he had a sensitive personality. However, it also confirmed one thing for us; we knew our son. My husband and I both answered the questions in the same manner.

The police report did not offer any answers, it only opened up more questions. If only the police would have seen the hazing as the crime it truly was. If they had handled it in a more timely fashion, perhaps the outcome would have been different. It may have left no time for further harassment. More importantly, it would have let Matt know that he was important. The police failed in my opinion because, they did not see it as a high priority, it was "just kids being kids" or a "rite of passage". And, how could a school district simply ignore what had been going on? Why didn't they send out warnings to both parents and students about the last day of school?

With the death investigation over, now came the hearings for the assault case. We had not received a copy of the incident report to review until 10 minutes before the hearing. Again, we were amazed at the detective work; the two eyewitnesses were not interviewed. The attackers were not interviewed until almost two months after the incident. A third attacker seemed to vanish from the report all together. It happened on a neighborhood street across from a home, and no one was asked if they had seen anything. Once the attackers confessed, the investigation was finished.

I would have to testify on Matt's behalf. I would have to stand face-to-face with Matt's attacker and his family. I am not a public speaker, but I knew I would have to be strong. In my fragile state, I would have to stand my ground. Every mother protects her child, and when your child dies, that protective bond does not die. In some ways, the bond strengthens. I am an easygoing person, but when it came to my child, I could not back down; I was now Matt's voice. I went over it again and again. The words had to be just right. How in a few short minutes could I explain who Matt was? What would I say to the young man who assaulted Matt? My hands shaking and my voice quivering, I stood there and said what I needed to say. I told them who Matt was, why he was special, and why no one has the "rite" to assault someone else for their own enjoyment. I do think our comments swayed the judge, but the final ruling was one year of probation. Unfortunately, no community service, like Matt had wanted.

After everything that had happened, we knew we still had to be Matt's voice. We needed to let others know the dangers their children face. If we did not say something, we would be as guilty as those who came before us, who said nothing. There comes a time when parents who have lost a child, or any person dealing with grief, must take our grief with us, or let our grief take us. We have seen the other side, and we choose to carry Matt and his message with us, wherever we go. We knew we could begin to make a change, and if we help one child, we, (including Matt), will have made a difference.

A Personal How-To Guide to Effecting Change
Matt's Legacy
By Matt's parents, Tammy and Kevin Epling

July to December of 2002 was a blur of tears, anger and unbearable pain as we tried to move forward. Life on the outside kept moving, the seasons changed and life went on. We made it through a few "firsts" without Matt: birthdays, holidays, and family events. Although every day was tough, I was determined to get up each day and face it as best I could. I didn't want to end up like others I had known who were stuck in their grief. I could not bear to carry this pain forever. Grief reminded me of a song I often sung with my preschool class... When travelers are confronted with a swamp that is too wide to go around, they can't go over it and can't go under it; they must trudge right through it, so I begin to trudge, to someday get to the other side. This was the adjustment period, time to become used to our new "normal". I hated it. Our family of four was now only three.

How could there still be all these unanswered questions? How could a young life be reduced to a police report, and neatly categorized simply as an "angry young man?" Yes, I believe Matt was angry, angry about being humiliated, angry about being betrayed. He had every right to be. Nevertheless, to be simply characterized and classified this way was wrong. So I continued to try to find answers in hopes of effecting change.

Hazing

Studies have shown that students who are victims of hazing show anger towards their attackers and many can have long lasting after effects. This can be profound, especially when the hazing is forced (some students actively involve themselves in hazing rites to gain acceptance into a group or club, fraternities for example. Even religious organizations are not immune. In a report by *Alfred University* on Hazing in America's schools, over 200,000 students connected a hazing experience with religion).

Everything I looked at led us back to the hazing, and I wondered...what did we miss? Not just Kevin (my husband) and I, but in the bigger picture, did the community miss something? Did something that had been tolerated for years, as a "rite of passage," play the key role in Matt's death?

Even the term "rite of passage" made me think, does anyone have the "right" to assault another person for his or her own amusement or benefit? As I read more excerpts from the *Alfred University* study (which was completed in 2000), I was amazed at how widespread this issue was among high school students:

- 43% of American high school students reported being subjected to humiliating activities.
- 71% of those subjected to hazing reported negative consequences such as getting into fights, fighting with their parents, hurting others, doing poorly in school, and other problems.
- 15% considered suicide.
- Students agreed that swifter response to hazing and tougher penalties would help deter hazing incidents.

How much had this changed since the study was completed?

Power and control

Hazing is a specific subset of bullying, but at the core, they are both about "power and control". One person has power and control, one person does not. It is hard to define when hazing is an assault and when repeated hazing becomes bullying. In our own efforts, we did not draw much distinction between subsets of bullying behavior, such as harassment and hazing; our activism was aimed at a comprehensive anti-bullying plan.

But specifically, was there more we needed to know about Matt's hazing? Just because Matt was 14, did not mean he did not deserve the same attention an adult would have received in a similar situation. How could the eyewitnesses never be interviewed? Why was the judge not tougher on the attackers? Why did the school do nothing? While I was thinking those thoughts, it seemed all the blame was coming back at us. The system made it appear to be Matt's fault and ours - it was so much easier to simply blame the victim and his family than it was to punish the attackers.

In my heart, I don't think Matt wanted to end his life, but perhaps instead, intended to make a cry for help. He wanted to end the situation he was placed in. But, he left no note. Matt was away from his dad for only 15-20 minutes. Perhaps he wanted to get out of going to the police station the next day, possibly afraid of retribution. We simply don't know. Only Matt and God know that answer. But in looking for answers, when I read more information on bullying/hazing and its connection to suicide, I became more convinced. When I communicated with other parents online, learned more, I was convinced all of the incidents tied together and resulted in Matt's suicide.

I remember seeing a report on A&E called "*Bullied to Death*" and it talked about "bullycide" cases in America. We ordered the DVD so we would have it to refer to. Evidence if you will. I wanted to reach out to these other parents. I wanted to find out if they felt like I did and how they survived. I thought, *how can this subject be profiled on a national program yet no one in our community raised or considered the possible connection between Matt's bullies and his death?* Nobody but us. We needed answers.

Raising awareness one step at a time
Still feeling lost and alone, we joined a support group for grieving children, which also had a parent group. We shared our pain with other parents as they did with us. I began to feel some peace from being able to reach out to others, and I knew I was not alone. Our support group referred us to people with the State of Michigan who were looking for parents to speak before the Michigan Death Review Board. This would be the first major public step in telling our story. I stood once again before a crowd exposing my pain to some who may not believe what we had to say. It was also an opportunity to help others and to talk about Matt. I miss so many things about Matt, and now, I love talking about him.

The Review Board was a special audience, because it was composed of those who really needed to hear our story, a mix of counselors, police, fire personnel, lawyers and the people on the front lines. Maybe by hearing what we went through they would go back and try a little harder, listen a little more intently, and perhaps become a part of the change. After speaking about Matt and the hazing, people approached me from the audience, all with a multitude of questions. It was hard to answer them. I was just learning myself. There were parents desperate to seek answers whose children were now being bullied and they were scared for them. There was a woman who said this is a problem in her school district and that there had been six teen suicides in the past year. *Six!*

Shortly after Matt's death, we talked with our neighbors and we organized East Lansing Cares (EL Cares), a grass roots organization of parents who wanted to make change within the schools and community based on what had happened. After a few months, this became a citywide group called Safe Schools/Safe Communities. It was hard for me to go to meetings because it brought everything back, sometimes too much, too fast.

But, my husband, Kevin, dove in and was determined to make change.

But it was evident after a few meetings that no one really wanted to find out what happened. They just wanted to move on. Kevin was actually asked not to attend the very first meeting, as his presence would "make other people feel uncomfortable". Well, they should have been uncomfortable; we were talking about the death of a child. If that wouldn't motivate them, what would? I think some saw Kevin simply as a grieving dad, looking to blame everyone. He was a parent's worst nightmare. A walking symbol of what they could no longer ignore. It was hard to watch my husband struggle with those early experiences; it took so much out of him. Why couldn't they see the extra pain it was causing him? I feared for his health. Was it worth it? In my heart, I could not bear the thought of losing him too.

There were times I wished he would stop going to the meetings, just give up, let them win, but he wouldn't – because if they won, the children lost, Matt lost all over again. He made a promise to Matt to make a difference. If any of these people had to live my life for just one hour, I know all of their policies would have changed in the second hour. But they couldn't or wouldn't put themselves in my shoes. Kevin told me of school personnel who never showed up even though meetings were specifically rearranged for them to attend, as well as the times he was omitted from speaking when he had the most powerful things to say, the times his comments were ignored...all were painful reminders of what we lost, and how difficult our crusade had become.

I didn't have the strength, yet, to fight in public, but I could talk with Kevin about what he was going through and help him formulate our plans. We did not want a simple band-aid solution, as others wanted. We had to look at the core and find out what was rotten. I could see the beginnings of bullying behavior within my own preschool classes. It is almost instinctive, inbred, but what if we began to alter that idea and actually change the culture? In fact, the Alfred survey points out that 27% of the respondents noted, "preventing hazing would only come with a change in culture."

Through all this, we met a bullying expert from Michigan State University, Glenn Stutzky, who knew exactly what we were talking about. He knew the dangers of bullying. In his work he determined that bullying is the most common form of violence in our schools today. We enlisted his help and support and were thrilled when he joined the effort. Coming from us, our calls for action were not taken seriously. Glenn's expertise helped galvanize the response. Without him onboard, we were just "grieving parents", but with him we were much more.

The community changes began in 2003 with three major events, a school assembly, a town hall forum, and increased attention on the last day of school. Still, people were unsure about all this. Some still believed that hazing/bullying can be a positive team/personality building experience, but not if the individual doesn't want to be a part of it. Yes, there is a line that should not be crossed. We needed more people to be aware of that line.

Before the town hall forum happened, the news was all about the incident in Chicago (2003) concerning a high school powder puff game. Until those girls were caught on tape, assaulting their fellow classmates with paint and feces, hazing wasn't real to some people. It was just kids having fun. When we saw that on the news and the attention it was getting, we knew some people were beginning to think differently. Even the news reports had the school saying there was nothing they could do, then back peddling four days later that they should have done something and will now be taking action. It brought the reality of hazing into the homes of America. I wondered, what if they had just told students the year before that hazing and bullying were inappropriate behaviors. Would Matt's hazing have happened at all?

The night of the first town hall forum arrived. Kevin, Glenn, our police Chief, and school administrators were there to speak. I was so happy when close to seventy people showed up for our first town hall forum on bullying. These people were interested and wanted to help. It was scheduled for an hour and a half; it went for two and a half. There have since been two others. And to think Kevin had been told by a school administrator at a prior meeting that no one would come, and parents were not interested in this topic.

Then there were the school assemblies, for both the middle school and the high school. I can still remember the day when Kevin came home from a meeting, very upset. They didn't want him to speak at the assemblies; I think they were afraid of what he'd say. After another few personal meetings, he was given the okay to speak, but they wanted to see what he was going to say first. The former superintendent actually asked Kevin to say there was no connection between Matt's death and the hazing. He refused because he believed that would be the wrong message to send to the students.

I attended the high school assembly. The police chief said that hazing would not be tolerated. It was a crime, and if caught there would be consequences. When Kevin spoke, you could hear a pin drop. Afterwards some students came to us and told us they had been bullied and harassed.

One girl, in tears, said she had been hazed the same way as Matt and had never told anyone. In a way, the floodgates had been opened. We managed to open a door that had been sealed because of simple fear and ignorance of what truth would come out.

We targeted that first district-wide assembly for the last day of school because this is when Matt's hazing took place. The police provided a greater presence not only around the schools but also in the communities. Parents were encouraged by the schools to come pick their children up. The community had begun to change. People were more aware of this type of behavior. Police were looking for it, the schools and parents were talking and the children felt better about it. This was the beginning of our "culture change," June 6, 2003, our own D-Day if you will.

A few days after the assemblies, my husband and I were walking downtown, and there was a group of boys walking ahead of us. One of them looked back at us, several times. Then he came over and said to my husband, "You're the guy that spoke at our school. Kevin nodded, and the boy said, "Thank you", and he went back to join his friends. I remember thinking that must have taken a lot of courage for that young man to come over. We knew if we could touch one life, we had done our job. That one comment, that one pure expression of thanks, gave us the additional strength to continue. We don't know that boy, we never saw him again, but we remember him every day and thank him for his kind words.

The schools began in-school training with an outside specialist who covered all aspects of bullying. Over the years, grades K-8 have been through the program. Now four years later, finally the high school is onboard. However, some students had already begun to make changes on their own. One of Matt's friends told us they had eliminated all forms of hazing on the women's swim team. This was a decision the students made. Parents and teachers continually let us know what they thought of the changes. One teacher noticed a difference in the incoming ninth grade class, perhaps because they had two years of awareness training at the middle school. A parent said her child was now having a better year, due to less harassment from his classmates.

In 2005, our city was seeking nominations for its "Crystal Award" program. The award honors those who have gone above and beyond to help better the community. I nominated Kevin for the award. He had stood up against so much, taken so much extra pain to make all of this change happen. Privately I supported everything he had done and now I needed to publicly support him. I called on neighbors, our friends and family to nominate him as well. I got the phone call that he was among the finalists and a panel of nominators now had to come in and tell the selection team why he deserved this. I wish I had thought to tape what people said, to play it back again. I didn't know the real impact he had made on people. My tears flowed along with the words being said. Kevin was selected as the recipient of the award, and accepted the award on behalf of the Safe Schools Safe Community group, and Matt. It was a truly emotional moment for us, but also bittersweet. We would certainly give up the award to spend another hour, minute, even a few seconds with our son. But still it was a meaningful, small victory we could claim in Matt's name.

Since that fateful night in July 2002, we have seen a monumental change and awareness in our community. To hear parents and students talk about the greater issue is encouraging. And our new police chief, as well as his officers, has re-prioritized their attention towards our young people's safety. We know a powerful seed has been planted. Looking back, we know many things were not done correctly by our local police, but now, by working with them rather than against them, we feel they are informed and trained to properly deal with this type of tragedy. With their help, we hope that no other student will face what Matt faced without being fully supported.

From changing a community to changing a State
Soon there were articles in the local papers and television stories about what we were doing. I remember the first TV story that came out. I was so nervous. I have always been a private person, now even more people would know our story. It was so hard to see those first images of Matt on TV. I was worried about what they might say. Would they stick to what we said? Would they portray Matt as he really was? How would it make our daughter feel? It wasn't easy, especially hearing the word "suicide" associated with his image, but we had to get our story out. This was our crusade.

A State legislator, who had seen our stories and had read about what we were doing, approached us. He said he was working on a new anti-bullying/harassment bill (Michigan had recently passed an anti-hazing bill). He wondered if we would be interested in telling our story in the committees and helping with the legislation. There was an anti bullying law already in the senate, but it was stuck in committee since 2001 because of the wording. We looked over the bill and added what we thought was necessary, based on what we had been through. We were touched when we were told, that when passed, it would be known as

"Matt's Safe School Law". The idea of Matt living on in a document, a law, to help others was at times overwhelming. This would be a small, but very significant part of Matt's legacy to others.

One of our proudest days was when my daughter, my husband and I stood next to our State Governor as she announced her support for the bill. She wore a picture of Matt on her lapel, as all of us on stage did. She talked about the bill, how important it was for the children of Michigan. She said all kids have the right to be safe at school. The co-sponsors of the bill spoke and noted that the bill had been introduced in both the house and the senate. My husband also spoke with strength and compassion. I never have been so proud.

Then the Lobby Day for our Bill came, I did not know what to expect. I had never been to a Lobby Day before. I was overwhelmed by emotion when we walked into the room. The room was overflowing with people, almost every seat was taken and people lined the walls. It was composed of a very diverse group of people from all walks of life. There were parents, family members and most of all, students. I was touched by all of the students there. Every person in that room wore a "Support Safe Schools, Pass Matt's Law" sticker. It hit me then, we had made it this far and for the first time we felt as if we were not avoided, but supported; and in fact, we felt honored.

My eyes kept shifting to a young man with the most amazing Mohawk I have ever seen. I couldn't help thinking how Matt would think that was so cool. As I looked around the room at the many faces from all across the state, I knew that this was what it is all about – these are the kids that had been bullied, hazed, and assaulted. Matt's law would help turn the tide. But, there were those who would be obstacles.

Later, when we were outside the senate chamber, the senator who was the Chair of the Education committee came out to speak with another parent (he was one of the afore-mentioned *obstacles*). I was amazed at his abruptness in how he spoke with her. She couldn't respond. I could not believe she was being bullied right in front of us. Kevin stepped in, introduced himself, and told him why the parents were there. Some had children who had been bullied, others like us, had lost a child. Amazingly, the senator was unfazed. In a matter of fact manner, he noted that there was no proof the bill was needed, and that it would not do any good even if it was passed. I showed him the picture of Matt we were wearing and the stickers the other parents wore. The senator still disagreed and gave excuses why they were not going to call a hearing. Kevin kept at him laying out the details and why it would help students.

I looked around and noticed a crowd was forming, people were gathering and Kevin kept hammering on the senator. Finally, I could see the senator was noticing the crowd too; he very quickly tried to wrap up the conversation by stating, "I'm not going to change your mind, and you're not going to change mine." I knew then that this would not be an easy victory, but we could not let one person's ignorance hold us back.

Keeping a legacy alive
Throughout all of this, it was important to us to keep Matt's legacy alive. This was all about Matt and who Matt was, not the person who died, but the person who lived and gave so much to those around him. I am reminded of the Japanese quote "Ask me how he died, and I will tell you how he lived."

After all we had done, to help make children safer in school, we still felt in some areas we were not embraced. When Matt passed away, we had a scholarship fund set up in his name. We thought his senior year would be the perfect time to use it. We envisioned a scholarship of the arts, something that would encompass all areas of art as Matt's talents did. We had talked to the school district the summer before school started to get the ball rolling. Kevin and I came back with a fully realized plan for a special kick-off event. We had designed invitations, t-shirts, and had local sponsors on-board. We even planned the "theme" for the event, an "afterglow" party after a school concert or play. We believed this "afterglow" event would allow Matt's classmates to be part of it as well as give them some closure to our shared loss. We hoped that this would be a recurring event to gather funds to support children in the arts for years to come.

We were surprised and hurt when the teachers eventually declined our idea. They wanted us to come up with something else. They gave some ideas but not one teacher stepped forward to assist and work with us, as we had no idea how things worked at the high school. We even talked with the student leaders and they too wondered why the teachers had said no. They really liked the idea and wanted to help any way they could. We waited for four months for a response from the school and time was running out. With what seemed like little support at the school level, it would be hard to start all over again. It was yet another painful blow. After all we had done for other kids, and only wanting to do more, to be turned away by the school was heartbreaking.

But like everything else we had been through, this additional pain opened another door for us. We began to think outside the box, what would Matt do? What did he love to do? It was simple, art. Although the art scholarship would not happen, we would honor Matt by creating an art competition in his name for other students at his Middle School. We approached our local art festival, went before the board of directors, and explained our idea. We wanted to give middle school children a venue to show their art in public, for them to be recognized alongside adult artists.

I held back the tears as they agreed. I was waiting for the "but" to come, but it never did. I was relieved. I knew this was such a tender age. We needed to give these students their own "showcase" to say they are special individuals just as Matt was. This would incorporate the schools, the city and the greater community, in one event. Both the School Board and City Council members also endorsed it.

One of the happiest of the bittersweet times was when a reporter came to our home, not to report on Matt's hazing or his death, but on what Matt was still giving to others. The "Matt Epling Creative Art Competition" was a reality! It came at just the right time, as in 2006, Matt would have been graduating from high school, another milestone we missed. As other parents planned open houses, we planned the art show. And it was met with great success! The art teacher at the middle school did a wonderful job of mounting the artwork. We had artwork from thirty-eight students, enough to fill a twenty by forty foot tent! We gathered close to five hundred votes for a single "People's Choice" award.

In all, five awards were handed out to the student artists. To see those students receive awards and share them with their parents was a wonderful experience. The only thing missing was Matt. If this opportunity had been available to Matt, he certainly would have participated.

We were also thrilled that the competition was honored by the Neighborhood Association of Michigan with its 2006 "Innovator Award" for community programs that filled a "special need or service." Our second art competition was in ways more successful than the first. The student who won the first "Judge's Choice" stopped by and informed us that her award and winning entry helped her get a scholarship to a special art camp for the summer. Another chapter in Matt's legacy, by helping other's we help ourselves.

We found that the ordeal we faced with the school was not uncommon. A student's death is a terrible thing; but a suicide doubles the anxiety on how to deal with the situation. We were not looking for Matt to get any special attention, only what he or any student should receive; respect. To us this was as much about Matt's classmates as it was Matt. We were pleased when the senior class held a tree planting ceremony in his memory. To us it not only symbolized closure for the school and Matt's classmates, but also the opening of a new door for acceptance and discussion.

So what is the point of telling you all of this? Well, there are several. First and foremost I am telling our story the best way I know how so that you might learn something; so that you might be inspired to make a difference or get involved in your own community; so that you might head-off some of the difficult things we've experienced. I think the details are important. Ours is a road map, just one possible route that can be taken to really effect change. I have also written these words, these many words, to honor my son. I thank you for indulging me in this; I'm sure if you were in my shoes, it would be important for you to do the same.

I offer my words as a plea. I do not want you to say, *it will never happen to me, not here, in our community, in my house.* - Because it can. In addition, don't believe that your schools or community would never respond; because they will, if you band together and make your wishes known. If not, bullying will continue to victimize children, and schools or communities will continue to sweep it under the rug. And as long as schools, police departments, parents and communities bury their heads in the sand, parents will continue to bury children. We parents, with a unified voice, can tell them that bullying and hazing not only hurts, it kills.

We have continued to share our story with other schools, civic groups, organizations and the media (most recently CNN) to help raise awareness. We are now waiting for our bill "Matt's Bill", to be reintroduced to the House and Senate. We are hopeful that 2007 will finally be the year that Michigan's children can begin to feel safer in their schools.

Update – On March 28th 2007, there was a second Lobby day for the anti bullying bill. Parents and children joined with our legislators for passage of the bill. Kevin presided over a press conference that included the sponsoring legislators and our Governor with a simple message "Pass Matt's Law"! The momentum was so great the bill was sent to the House floor that afternoon and was passed 50-59. We are now awaiting a hearing in the Senate to finally pass "Matt's Safe School Law".

Our talks to community groups have broadened beyond bullying to help those with their grief and how they can channel it into productive ways. We have seen the basis of the Safe School Safe Community copied by other communities as the awareness level across the state grows. Kevin is now working with the State Police and others to help create a K-12 anti-bullying curriculum for police officers and we continue to assist other parents whose voices are not heard.

Kevin's Postscript (Tammy's husband gives an update)
I have been working with a group of law enforcement officers here in Michigan to create a K-12 curriculum for police officers on anti-bullying tactics. On Wednesday, we had our first training session – we thought we would have 40-60 officers attend; we had close to 130 from departments across the state.

I kicked off the day with Matt's story, followed by Glenn Stutzky M.S.W., (national expert in bullying), a funding resource officer for the state and then two officers who worked on the curriculum.

During the middle of the day, an officer whom I have met before came up to me and told me a story.

A student at his school told him about a fellow student who had sent a text message stating "Thanks for being a friend I won't be around tomorrow"

This officer knew the person and grabbed another officer and went to the student's home.

His parents where gone and he broke down and said that he had attempted to kill himself.

The officer told me that 2 years ago he would have never responded the way he did. But by hearing our story and attending other seminars he looks at things very differently now, and in turn he said WE saved a life that day.

So yes, in our own ways we are making a difference. You can change the world, or your own corner of it.

Note: In early December 2011, after many years of trying, Kevin Epling and the Michigan lawmakers he had been working so hard with, finally passed **Matt's Safe School Law**, in honor of Kevin's son, Matt Epling.

8 Months to Bullycide

"Bullies WILL cause depression and depression is the number one cause of suicide. The signs are there – be aware!"

April's Story

In loving memory of April Himes
4/27/86 – 2/14/00
By Summer Himes

I am the mother of four children, Marlena, Scotty, Gregg and April. My youngest daughter, April, is forever 13 years of age, as she now lives with God. It has only been within this last year, that when asked about my children, I include her. How does a mother explain in a short and polite way that a child has chosen to leave the family, by suicide? Nevertheless, April's memory is with us and in our hearts.

April loved her family and friends and there was a time that April loved her life and living. It seemed that April wanted to try everything life put before her. However, that all began to change just eight months before the worst day of our lives.

Before I tell you about April's worst eight months, I would like to tell you about her as a person.

She was very friendly. There was not a shy bone in her body. April was older and wiser than many of her friends. I think that is why she had such good friends. April loved all animals. She had a pet lovebird named George. Her bird would jump down to the floor and run into her bedroom when April came home from school. That was the sweetest thing to watch. We had to have his wings clipped; otherwise he would have flown to her wherever she went. April's bird would crawl in her shirt and all you could see was his head peeking out at you. He was very content and happy when he was with April.

George died a few months after April did. No one knows why George died so suddenly, but I believe he died of a broken heart.

April loved to play with our poodles. She loved to help me cook at Thanksgiving and Christmas. She could make an awesome pecan pie. She liked skating and ice sledding. She had a lively and contagious spirit about her. And these things are just the tip of the iceberg. I wish I could help you to know her as I knew her before those last eight months of her life, so you can love her and understand that the April I know is not the April that left us.

June 1999
Our family moved to Richland, Washington, very near our former home. April would soon begin the eighth grade. In her former school, April's grades were A's and B's, she had flown through the end of the seventh grade with no problems. As summer began in her new house, she was missing her old friends. So she invited her best friend to sleepovers, and they would call each other all the time.

September
Summer went by very fast and school began at the end of August. There were a few girls that April knew from before, but she had never really been friends with them. As the new girl in school, April became very lonely in her new environment. Her peers were very distant and didn't embrace her as her former friends had.

I quickly began to see a difference in April. During this first month, the bright lights in her eyes were dimming. She was acting differently. She did not come home with a smile, nor did she laugh as much anymore. She stopped listening to music. She stopped singing. Little by little, she was changing. She was not the same happy-go-lucky girl anymore.

She would talk to me about a few problems with some girls at school, but she always minimized the issues. I tried to give her hope and told her to stick with it, to give the girls a chance to get to know her. I told her to, "Be yourself and they will come around." April seemed to cheer up after our talks; at least, that's what I thought.

I noticed that April was not sleeping as much as she used to. My husband, her stepfather, would leave the house around 3 a.m. to go to work, and April would often climb in bed with me after he left. Sometimes we would talk, sometimes not. I really miss that special time we shared. And I only wish I had seen it for what it was—a sign of things to come.

One September morning, when it was time to get up and go to school, April confided to me that she had taken 40 ibuprophen. I quickly sat up and asked "Why?" She said she was depressed. I called a friend and we went to the hospital. They ran tests and concluded the medicine did not affect her liver. Physically she was okay, but mentally, she was not.

April had waited eight hours before telling me about the pills. That sent shivers down my spine. I knew that I couldn't protect my little girl all the time; that I couldn't have stopped her from doing such a thing. I will never forget that moment, that realization. The doctor strongly suggested that April enter a mental health facility to get some counseling.

This pill-popping (overdose) incident was not an accident. April knew about my bi-polar illness, as we had talked it over before. Because of my depression, I had spent some time in the hospital myself. I was able to explain the process to April. I gave her an idea of what it would be like and how it had helped me. She wasn't angry or scared, and volunteered on her own to go, although it threw her for a huge loop when they said they wanted her to go "that very minute".

I stayed calm for April until I got home, and then I felt as if a stake had pierced my heart — April could have died and I didn't see it coming. I was so upset with myself. Of all people, I should have known because I have been there. The signs were there. ... She wasn't sleeping, she wasn't herself, she was eating more than usual and she was having at least two headaches a week. It should have been a loud and clear wake-up call.

October
April was in the mental health facility for about two weeks. She was quiet the first week. She listened during the meetings but would not participate. She was put on a low dose of an antidepressant. The second week in the facility she caught up on her homework and started loosening up. She was participating in all the activities. She was learning the tools to help her cope in different situations. April told me that in the group sessions she would tell them some of the things that were going on in school. Then the group would role play what she had just explained to them. The counselor would then step into her shoes and show her a better way to handle that particular situation.

April felt she was getting good at handling the verbal role-plays and she seemed happier and more relaxed. Soon April felt she was ready to go back to school. And she seemed to believe in herself again.

I called April's school and talked to the principal about everything that was going on. I wanted him to know where April had been and why. I told him to talk to her teachers also. I figured that if they knew what was going on they would be able to watch over her and help her if she needed it.

April was worried about what to tell her friends, about where she had been. Understandably, she did not want to tell her friends the truth, so I suggested that she tell her friends that she had a family emergency. She left that morning with a huge smile on her face. She did not come home in the same condition.

After school, April came home crying and throwing up. A teacher had betrayed the confidential knowledge we had entrusted in her about where April had been and why. My daughter was devastated. The consequences of this one unprofessional act destroyed two weeks in counseling. The news was all the motivation classmates needed to begin tormenting April. April did not go back to school for eight days. She was emotionally and physically sick and there was nothing I could say that would comfort her.

I felt I had let April down. How could I have known that her teachers would hurt her — even if they did not mean to — with their gossip. I was heartbroken.

November
The bullying that had started recently was now getting worse, and April would only tell me a few things that were happening. It was more than one bully now. One pushed her against her locker. Another student was throwing pencils at her in class. Her teacher saw what was going on but did nothing. April said she looked at him with begging eyes to do something, but, incredibly, he did nothing.

April went on and off to school. She was failing her classes. She couldn't keep up with her homework. She had given up. We were at a loss to find a way to help her. The mental health treatment backfired when it was supported inappropriately at school. We just didn't know what to do.

December
During the Christmas holiday, her friend, Annie, took her skiing with their family. I was so glad. April smiled, laughed and seemed happy again. They had a great time. They videotaped her. We enjoyed watching how much fun she had. She was happy for a week after that.

One morning, April slipped into bed with me again. This time, instead of sharing difficult school experiences, she told me she had started her period. With pride I said, "Welcome to womanhood."

January 2000
April could not wait to tell her friends about starting her period. It was

an important event in her life. She had gone to school that whole week and I was hopeful that the other girls had tired of the bullying and would finally accept her in their group. Then, the last day of the week, April's friends were talking to her about her period. They wanted to know how it felt. Unfortunately, the main bully heard about April's big moment and began to spread a rumor that April stuffed her bra with toilet paper, even adding more insulting comments about her having acne and being overweight.

The second week April stayed home for a few days with a headache. One evening my husband, April and I were out together. April went into a store and was gone less than a couple minutes when she came back to the car, slammed the door and said, "Hurry, let's go home!" I was dumbfounded. What could have happened?

When we arrived at home, April told us she had seen her entire group of "friends", including the one who instigated all the bullying. They said they were all having a sleepover and she wasn't invited. The bully then asked April if she knew why she wasn't invited, but before April could answer, the bully told her that she was not invited because she was not one of their friends. All of her friends just stood there and said nothing. April tried to look at her best friend in the group but she was looking at the floor. April was humiliated. The only thing she could do was run.

How can one person have so much control over a whole group? Where does that power come from and why? Why don't friends stick up for other friends in such situations? How does it spin out of control unchecked? It would be fascinating to consider, if it weren't so dangerous, and deadly. The next day at school, April's best friend apologized to her, but the damage had been done. Trust had been broken. April's self-worth had taken a huge blow.

February
Her tormentors were really having a field day with April, and she was getting very sick. She wasn't eating, sleeping or watching TV. She was just lying around the house, always sick to her stomach or suffering from a headache. I gave her Tylenol for her headaches but she was going downhill – physically and emotionally – very rapidly.

April was telling us everything that was going on now, and it was *not* insignificant. My husband called her school counselor and repeated what April had told us. He asked the counselor if she would meet with April and try to help her. The next day April was called out of her classroom to visit with the counselor. Later, the counselor called my husband and was very angry. She had thought it was April's idea to talk to her, but instead April was very hostile. The counselor yelled at my husband and said she would never talk to April again. We were incredulous. She knew all the details. Knew it was serious. Didn't she have a responsibility to break through to her? All we wanted was to get just one person on April's side at school. Clearly, disappointingly, it would not be the counselor.

One morning, after April had gone to school, I walked by her bedroom and something caught my eye. I saw a letter on top of her purse. I think I did what every other mother would do, especially given her fragile state. I read the letter. In her letter, April commented that she had done something that I would be upset about. I was very concerned and told my husband. We decided to confront April about it. She didn't deny what was in the letter but was angry with me for reading it.

The next day was April's meeting with her mental health counselor. Before beginning, April said she wanted to talk to her counselor alone. I knew she was still upset about the letter. When her counselor asked us to join them he expressed April's concern that her private space was violated.

I told him I read the letter because April was not talking to me, I didn't know what was going on with her and because I knew she was suicidal. I thought I might learn something from her letter that I could help her with. It was a fine line I was walking...violating my child's trust but I was looking out for her safety and her life. I knew it.

I was astounded when the counselor ignored what I said and repeated himself about April's privacy. I looked at him again and said, "Did you hear what I said? April is suicidal!" I was shocked when he ignored me again. What is more important, a child's privacy or that she is suicidal? He then responded he had already asked April if she was suicidal and she had told him that she was not. He believed April and felt that her privacy was a more important issue. Everywhere we turned for help it seemed answers were absent.

Since the counselor did not seem to understand what his job was, or the severity of the situation, I decided that the meeting was over and we left. When we got home, I immediately took all the pills in the house and hid them downstairs as her room was upstairs; there was no reason for her to be down there. I *knew* she was going to try to kill herself again. I was determined that was not going to happen. I felt that in my home I would have everything under control.

But I was getting no help from April's school and now, on top of that, I wasn't getting help from her mental health counselor. I was alone and scared. My husband and I were running out of options.

One morning, the beginning of the second week of February, I received a call from the principal at April's school. He asked if I knew April had missed 53 days of school. I said "yes". I reminded him that April had been in the mental health facility for two weeks and that she continued to have emotional and physical problems that keeping her from going to school. He said "okay", and then hung up. Once again, no help.

February 14, 2000 – Valentine's Day
Like every other morning, I ate breakfast and got on the Internet. I woke up April and told her she had to go to school as she did not have a headache or stomach ache. Her brother Gregg heard us arguing about going to school. He also wanted to stay home from school but I would not let him.

When April did not appear to be getting ready for school, I mentioned to my husband that I had received a disturbing phone call from the principal a few days prior, and that I was concerned April would have to repeat seventh grade. He said he understood and then went to talk to April. He asked her to go to school and suggested we would all talk that night. She was not interested. She was crying and very upset, and ran to her room and slammed the door.

Again, I knew that she was suicidal, but she was home. We were home. And she was safe – I had hidden all the pills. I tried to talk to April again, but she was crying and yelling at me to get out of her room. I didn't know what to do. I told April I was going to call the school. She said nothing.

I could not get a hold of the principal so I talked to the vice principal. I told him that I could not get my daughter to go to school. I asked him what he would suggest that I do. He said if she didn't come to school that he would be forced to fill out the Becca Bill form. I got quiet for a minute. What - I was confused? I'm asking for help and he is threatening me with some kind of form? What is going on here? After some silence on the phone, the vice principal explained that the Becca Bill required that the truant child go in front of a truancy board and tell them why they refused to go to school. Then the truant child could possibly spend some time in detention jail ("juvie") and maybe have to do some community service. I told him okay and then hung up. Community service was the least of my concerns at this point. But perhaps I could use it to motivate April.

I called April out of her room and told her what I was told. She yelled, "I can't believe you called the school." She went back in her room and slammed the door. After about ten minutes she come out of her room and asked me to repeat what the vice principal had said. I again repeated what I was told. At the time, it felt strange. It was as if she needed to verify what she had been told. It was a bizarre exchange, not the type of interaction we had before. She was crying and I was crying. She then yelled, "I hate you." Those are the last words I heard from April. The *last* words I ever heard from my daughter. Can you imagine?

Obviously, the "school today" issue was over. I lost that one. I thought she needed time for herself, so I left her alone. I did not hear a peep from April for three hours. But I *knew* she was safe. Even though I couldn't watch her all the time, every minute of every day, at least I *knew* she was safe right now.

My older daughter Marlena came over to talk with April as she sometimes did. Marlena went into April's room and found her sister hanging from her bunk bed, with a belt around her neck. I called 911, but I knew she was already dead.

She was not safe after all. My worst fear and nightmares had come true.

April had been crying for help and no one could or would listen. Her mental health counselor called when he had heard the news and asked if there was anything he could do? I told him there wasn't anything he could do *now*. I really wanted to tell him I had begged for his help but he had turned me down. What good would that do now, to put blame on anyone? I said nothing.

Later, the principal called my husband and told him that his vice principal denied saying anything about the Becca Bill to us. I guess we weren't surprised. The school would take no responsibility to help my daughter before her death, and it certainly would not take any responsibility after her death.

The "what if" questions still haunt me. What if Marlena had stopped by earlier? What if Gregg had stayed home that day? What if Scotty had called her that day? What if I had never called the school? What if I hadn't tried to make her go to school that day? And the biggest question of all – what if the school had cared and wanted to help April on that Valentine's Day? There are millions of "what ifs", and it doesn't make a difference anymore, nothing will change. April is gone from our lives.

April's funeral was held at our church. The place was packed. There were so many people there to show their support and how much they had loved April. My three beautiful children sang "A Child's Prayer" in her honor. It was so beautiful, like angels singing. I know without a doubt that April heard them. I believe with all of my heart that there is life after death. I believe she hears and sees us every day. She is with us, always with us.

It is my goal in sharing my story, April's story, that those reading it will learn from our experiences. I have been crying for days and days while writing and editing this. I have shed more than a few tears for every word I have written. I have reopened a huge wound. I thought was healed. To share this is something I need to do for me – definitely for April, but also for you. I am begging you to remember my daughter and others who have chosen that same path, not only for who they were, but because they can be great teachers; truly angels. They can save lives. Please understand that suicide is not an answer, it is only the end of life and the beginning of an even greater pain for those left behind. Please, do not let your children find this path.

I wrote this poem a month after April passed away.

MY DAUGHTER'S DEATH

My heart is open for the world to see.
My tear ducts open and flow free.
My soul aches from the pain of it all.
My Savior helps me stand tall.
Helping me knock down that fake and lonely wall.
My memories of her come and go in pieces.
April's puzzle of life ceases.

Summer Himes

The Pain of Depression
What it Feels Like
By April's mom, Summer Himes

I would like to put an end to a myth. I have heard that suicide is a very selfish act and that those who die by suicide are only thinking about themselves. This is so far from the truth. A person that takes his/her life by suicide is not thinking of themselves, or anyone else. A depressed and suicidal person is not *thinking* - the brain is not functioning well enough to have any rational thoughts. There are only feelings. It's all about emotions. You *feel* sad, upset, unloved, despair, hopeless, helpless, alone, gloomy, weighted down and rejected. These are just a few of the *feelings*.

What is Depression in the medical sense?
Depression is a very serious medical condition. It is a mood disorder. Don't confuse it with life's ups and downs. Life is stressful. Your boyfriend or girlfriend just dumped you or you got your first speeding ticket or even lost your job. You find a way to cope with the stressors in your life and then move on. The problem is when you can't cope with these stressors. The sadness, hopelessness and helplessness...when they last over a period of two weeks or more, then depression can creep into our lives. I think of it as a spider web that weaves itself in and around the brain. The illness changes your moods and the way you think. You can't concentrate or make intelligent decisions about everyday issues. Your feelings are negative and distorted. Depression takes root in work, school, family, social time, appetite, sleep, and in favorite activities.

Who gets Depression?
The answer is... Anyone. It can affect all ages, genders, income levels and faiths. Some depression may have genetic roots, but beyond that, we're a long way off from being able to tell who might be at risk.

What causes Depression?
Depression can come from many sources. It could be hereditary, a chemical imbalance, fluctuating hormones, or a stressful event or events in your life (a "trigger"). The event could be a breakup, a conflict within your family, death of a family member or friend, a car accident, the loss of a pet, or as in April's case, by peers bullying her at school. When someone is clinically depressed, the sadness lingers on and on, and it becomes debilitating.

What are the symptoms of Depression?
A person with Depression may only have two or three symptoms...or ten. You may suffer from Depression if you:

- Sleep all day or not to sleep at all
- Eat significantly more or less, gain or lose significant weight
- Have debilitating headaches
- Are restless, irritable, agitated
- Are Fatigued
- Have feelings of hopelessness, helplessness and despair
- Find it hard to concentrate and make decisions
- Are feeling unworthy or guilty
- Cry all the time...seemingly about *nothing*
- Have a lot of anger
- Are talking about or thinking about suicide

What does it feel like to be depressed?
As one who has lived with depression, think of all the emotions and feelings mentioned above and then think about feeling these all at the same time and multiplies infinitely. These are the darkest and heaviest moments of your life. Your emotional feelings become physical. By that, I mean my soul was feeling tortured. It hurt so bad I couldn't breathe. It felt like my soul was being stretched and squeezed out of my body. There is no stopping it. It is bigger than life itself. You cannot control it. It controls you. That moment of time seems to last forever. When I'm depressed, I am so engulfed in these moments of feelings that I seem to fall in a dark and eerie hole. I know, I believe, there is no way out because of all those negative feelings.

What's real and what's not real?
When I am depressed, there were times that I feel like I am becoming part of a bottomless hole, but then sometimes, by the Grace of God, the phone will ring. It takes a moment to return to reality. My best friend calls. I have no idea what we talk about or how long but when I get off the phone I would notice that there were two bottles of pills in my lap. I don't know why I picked up those pills or when I had gotten up to go get them. Again, lucid, clear thoughts are hard to come by in these moments...While writing April's story for this book I actually had one of these episodes.

I have bi-polar illness. This is when a person has extreme lows and extreme highs. I only have highs maybe twice a year. The rest of the time I'm fighting depression. At times, my life is like a rollercoaster. Up and down. I take medicine to help me find balance. A middle ground.

Before she died, April was diagnosed with Depression. She was taking an antidepressant to battle it. I would ask her all the time if she felt it was helping. She always said "no". Would another medicine have worked? Who knows? I personally do not think anyone under the age of 18 should be put on antidepressants, but I am not blaming the antidepressant for April's death. The bullies triggered April's depression. And depression led to her suicide. I know the antidepressant did not help her. But if it did hurt her, I'm convinced it was only a minute problem. I compare it to one drop of water in a half filled bathtub.

What are the Warning Signs of Depression?

- Making suicidal statements
- Giving away belongings
- Withdrawing from family and friends
- Failing grades
- Doing less of what used to give them pleasure
- Becoming emotionally or physically upset for no reason
- Hostility
- Preoccupation with death

Can Depression be treated?
Yes. A doctor can diagnose Depression. Several things can happen. The doctor may prescribe medication, likely, an antidepressant. Children on antidepressants should be closely monitored. Experts disagree on the safety of such medications for younger people. There are a variety of different antidepressant drugs, and one may provide better relief for a patient than others. Medical treatments for depression should be carefully considered and discussed with a doctor; this means that regular visits to the doctor should be made to follow-up and possibly "tweak" the medication to fit the individual needs of the child. Don't leave everything up to the doctor. You must take control of the situation and take action. You must observe your child and then talk with the doctor.

Ongoing therapy and counseling is another great source of aid for people with depression. In addition, a support network of friends and families is a vital part of treating chronic depression. Isolation and withdrawal are common symptoms of depression. Please consult the resources in the end of this book for more solutions to chronic depression.

My final words... Don't give up hope. Depression can be treated!

Recipe for a Disaster

"If you think something is wrong, something is probably wrong. Go with your gut feelings"

Kristina's Story
Nice Girls Finish Last Too

In loving memory of Kristina Arielle Calco
12/26/89 – 12/4/05
By Michelle Calco

One blustery snowy morning in December 2005, we awoke to find that our 15-year-old daughter, Kristina Calco, had abruptly ended her own life.

Kristina had been approaching her 16th birthday with an excitement which was barely containable. Yet, for some reason unbeknownst to us at the time, this beautiful young girl, who on the surface seemed to have just about everything going for her, felt the need to check out of life for good.

This is the Eulogy that I wrote and read at Kristina's visitation:
My daughter was a very sensitive young girl of 15 who sadly was just never meant to make it to her 16th birthday, which would have been 12/26/2005.

To us and everyone else, this Saturday, (December 3, 2005) seemed not much different from any other Saturday. Kristina slept in, ate breakfast, showered and dressed. She asked to go to the library to get books for a project she was working on about John F. Kennedy. I dropped her off at the library while I drove to pick up her sister from dance class. After that, I drove Kristina to the mall to do some shopping. She was helping her friend get ready for the dance, and decided that she would like to go after all. When she came home, she went directly upstairs to fix her hair. When she was done with her hair and makeup, we drove to get a dress at Marshall Fields. She chose the dress she wanted, we paid and we cut the tags so she could wear it out.

We drove home to get the $10 dance entrance fee and my husband. Kristina asked me how she looked, to which I replied that she looked great, which of course wasn't what she wanted to hear. She had wanted me to tell her that she looked beautiful, which of course she did. Kristina told us the dance was over at 11 pm, so my husband arrived shortly after that to pick her up. He called her cell but she told him she had made an error and that it was really over at 11:30. She came out sometime around 11:40 PM, came home, showed the other kids in our family her dress, and proceeded to get on AOL Instant Messenger (AIM). I must have told her six times to take off her dress and get ready for bed. She asked me to take her picture first, which did not seem an unusual request as she did this for every dance she attended. I took her picture and then went up to bed.

That's the last time I saw Kristina alive.

We later found out that she had been on AIM and MY SPACE until at least 2 am, maybe longer.

We, like many parents in this tragic situation, were left to pick up the pieces. Fortunately for us, in addition to two suicide notes, Kristina left behind page after page of detailed journal entries, dozens of MYSPACE personal emails and numerous AOL Instant Messenger Conversation screen prints. We are now able to piece together a timeline for Kristina, which begins with bullying and teasing from at least the 7th grade on.

The Suicide Note
Our first indication of what had happened was found in Kristina's suicide note, which was written in the form of a poem. She wrote:

"I knew I was always the ugly one.
Don't say that's a lie
Because you don't know, what some kids have said and done.
It hurts to think about how mean some people could be.
Even when I started to look a little better,
They still couldn't see."

We were absolutely dumbfounded! Not only could we not make heads or tails of it, but also we had absolutely no idea why she would write that. She had blossomed into such a beautiful girl.

In addition to having feelings of being horribly unattractive, Kristina wrote too, that she was extremely sad and alone and hurt. Yet, Kristina would never want anyone to take on any of her pain. In her suicide note, she felt the need to constantly reiterate how sorry she was and that she didn't want anyone to have to live with any sort of guilt. This was going to be her decision, her choice and her fault. She wanted everyone to know that they had all touched her life in ways that she would never ever forget. She wanted everyone to know that she loved them all so very much and that they were all such wonderful and amazing people. She wanted to let everyone know that she would always be with them and be in their hearts. She was thankful that everyone had been so good to her.

The Search for Answers

We began our search for answers with MySpace.com and with AOL Instant messages.

Initially, we found two Instant Message Conversations in which Kristina said to a friend, "You should have heard what they said to me in middle school. It was awful. I felt like crying. Everyday this boy would tell me I was ugly and nasty, and then he got other people to say it too. It was torture and a living hell."

In another IM conversation, she tells another person, "Everyone I've ever liked has always rejected me for reasons of 'God, you are so ugly' or 'I'd never go out with you'."

When the other party questioned her, about whether these words were actually spoken to her and what she did about it, Kristina replied, "Yes, they actually said those words to me and I cried a lot."

What friends said

We began to question her group of friends, which included both her middle school friends as well as her High School friends. Yes, it was all true, Kristina was teased and tormented and ridiculed throughout her middle school years and up to at least the 9th grade. Neither she nor any of her friends ever told a single adult about what was going on. We were told that there was a particular group of boys that did this to her and that every day the girls would have to console Kristina in the cafeteria. Her friends would reassure Kristina that she was not ugly and that she was beautiful.

Unfortunately, the bullying never ended. Kristina, who was such a frail and sensitive girl, was made to feel ugly on a daily basis by a group of her own peers. By the time she was in the 9th grade, she had internalized the verbal assaults until she believed them with every grain of her soul.

A friend wrote about Kristina, "*there was something about her that just made the entire room light up. She exuded radiance and had a sparkling personality that led others to feel better without warning. She was one of those rare gems that was as gorgeous on the inside as she was on the outside. She was incredibly multitalented, intelligent, and articulate, and she had a certain grace and class to her that was lacking in many others her age.*"

Kristina cared about everyone, to the detriment of even herself. She was kind and considerate, caring, and always made people feel so good about themselves. Kristina worried about her friends, her bullies, and the world around her. She wrote about her deep desire to help humanity in some way and that it was her hope to become a great scientist and find a cure for Cancer and for AIDS.

Changes at home

At home, Kristina's shy and quiet personality gradually changed during those crucial Middle school years. She never told on her bullies. She never would let us inside her own private world of suffering. We began to see someone who was never happy, and nearly always angry about one thing or another. Her self-image suffered terribly. She began to see herself as ugly and she outwardly expressed this to us on what now looking back seems to have been a daily basis. It never mattered what we or anyone else said.

We told ourselves that Kristina's behavior was her 'normal' progression through teenage life. After all, she had always been so shy and had worried about things beyond her years from such a young age.

We now realize that because of what was happening to Kristina at school, and since she did not have an outlet for her feelings, she expressed them openly without hesitation when amongst her family members. Unfortunately, we did not recognize Kristina's behavior as depression. When we look back at her journals, we can now see that she had been suffering from depression for a very, very long time.

Kristina's Journal

Kristina Arielle Calco wrote about herself in the summer before 7th grade...

"Hi, I'm Kristina Calco and I'm 12 ½ yrs old going on 13 on Dec. 26 (the day after Christmas aren't I lucky?) You are reading about my life in my preteen/teenage years. Let me tell you a few things about me. I have wavy/curly dark brown hair an inch or two longer than my shoulders and dark...and brown eyes. I wear glasses and am a little pale, not so much anymore because I got tan over the summer. I'm 4 ft 10 ½ (I know I'm short for my age, 20th percentile, but I'm growing.) I'm in 7th grade this year and am dying to be 13 (then I'll finally be a teenager!). I have to get braces really soon & right now I'm wearing a twin block to move my jaw forward. I had an overbite but it's almost gone because my treatment for that will be over soon. Although braces are no walk in the sun, they've got to be better than this! I'm not popular but I'm not a loser and I'm actually pretty shy around other kids, unless I know them well."

In middle school, Kristina was a 4.0 honor student who always strived for perfection in everything she did. She was extremely artistic and her work was chosen not only to be on the cover of the school yearbook but she was also selected to design the school t-shirts. In an effort to overcome her shyness, she joined the student broadcasting staff, the yearbook staff and the newspaper staff. Although she was admittedly not the best at sports, she joined the Swim team, the Volleyball team, the Track team and even joined the Ski Club. She signed up for Forensics and earned a 3rd place trophy in the 2003 State Forensics Tournament. She later wrote that no one would ever know how hard that was for her. That was actually one of the proudest moments of her life. Kristina supported her school in every way imaginable and attended numerous sporting events, such as basketball and football. At the end of the 8th grade, Kristina tried out for and made the JV Cheerleading team for High School. She wrote in her journal, *"Me, Kristina Arielle Calco, I made the cheerleading squad for high school! JV too! I'm so proud of myself!"*

Despite all of her accomplishments however, some would choose to drag Kristina down.

Kristina was maturing and going through puberty, as well as dealing with the pressures of getting good grades at school, peer pressure, and of course dealing with boys. In addition to the typical pressures that every teenager has, Kristina placed a lot of additional pressure on herself.

We found in her journal that she had made some goals for herself, that before she was sixteen, *"Everything would be perfect.... I would be gorgeous & have perfect hair & teeth & clothes & I'd have a boyfriend & I would have had my 1st kiss & I would be popular & have awesome shoes & be really thin & tall and all of the boys would wanna get with me & I'd be on Varsity Cheerleading & do Volleyball and have sweet abs & skinny thighs & fit into Abercrombie pants and be rich and ya know I'd be sooo happy & have a 4.0 still, and ya know if that doesn't happen I told myself I'd have to kill myself. I know how I'm gonna do it too...but nevermind for now...."*

Kristina mentioned suicide in her journals many times dating back at least as far as January 2005 (almost a year before her December death).

Outwardly, Kristina put on a happy face. She had the kindest, biggest heart, and in her journal expressed that she could never be cruel to anyone and could never understand in her sweet 15-year-old mind, how people could be so mean to other people. She said it actually 'caused her pain' to see that. She told me about going to parties where everyone seemed so out of control. She told me about how she tried drinking and how she hated the feeling, and swore she would never do it again. She told me that she felt guilty. I told her that nearly everyone tries it and that she did not have to participate in anything she didn't feel was right. After all, everything in life is a choice.

Kristina always wanted to be the "good girl" that she thought she ought to be. She had such high expectations for herself. On the other hand, she would never fault other people for the choices that they made. She would never judge anyone else. She just simply chose to extract herself from those situations. She had standards for herself as well as standards that she imagined others had of her.

But paired with these high standards, was Kristina's extremely low self-esteem. She wrote in her journal about a girl that she admired. Some girl that was 'really pretty and really nice, too' and how every time that she saw her, the girl would smile at her. *'Isn't that nice,* she wrote'. *"Everyone likes her. I wish I was like that."* Kristina did not realize that to everyone else, she was that girl. She wrote, *"I just pretend I look really good. Sometimes it's really hard though, because I don't like lying ...thinking that I'm pretty when I'm not.'*

The last few weeks
In the last few weeks, a lot happened in Kristina's life. Things that were on her 'to-do' list, (from her earlier journal entries), just were not materializing the way that she had so hoped they would. In her eyes, everything wasn't perfect... she wasn't gorgeous, she didn't have perfect hair, teeth, and clothes and she didn't have a boyfriend. She wasn't popular and didn't have awesome shoes and wasn't really thin and tall and couldn't see that all of the boys probably did want to get with her ...and she hadn't made the Varsity Cheerleading team ...and she hadn't made the Volleyball team ...and she didn't have sweet abs and skinny thighs ...and she didn't fit into Abercrombie pants...and she wasn't rich and she definitely wasn't happy. In Kristina's minds' eye, about the only thing she did have was the 4.0. She didn't see the treasure that she really was. For Kristina, typical teenage pressures, combined with her self-imposed pressures, eventually consumed her.

For whatever reason, in the wee morning hours of Sunday December 4th, Kristina lost her focus. The stage had been set and with such a frail and sensitive soul, she just could not bear the pain that had consumed her. In that one tiny infinitesimal instant, Kristina made the choice to kill herself. Suicide seemed her only escape, her only way out, her only way to end the pain.

You see, in Kristina's mind, life was like a test where there was supposed to be a perfect outcome. She was always looking for a certain set of steps to follow, a clear and precise beginning, middle and end, and life just doesn't conform to those rules, despite all the wishful thinking in the world. For Kristina, it was like trying to solve a math equation for which she had been given the wrong formula from the start. No matter what she did, she just couldn't get the correct answer.

I believe that if Kristina had truly known the devastation that her death would bring, she would never, ever have done it. I am certain that she could not possibly have really wanted to die. This young, naïve 15 year old girl with a romantic image of what she had by this point trivialized...Suicide...made a fateful decision in what seems to be the heat of a single solitary moment in time. She wanted her pain to end and as she saw it, this was her only way out. Kristina was such a bright girl, but she had set her goals so very, very high, that they were simply unattainable by anyone including herself.

Kristina could never have understood the finality of what she did. She wrote about it so often as if she could have done it any day or time, just as you or I would take a breath. I know that in her mind she imagined it would be like simply walking away down a long road and just not coming back. In my heart, I know that she couldn't possibly have fully realized how one person's life could touch so many people's lives. She didn't understand that once you are gone, you can never, never, ever, come back.

As tragic as our story is to tell and live each day, I feel there are things to be learned from Kristina's story and what a teenage girl goes through. Kristina wrote in a 7th grade journal entry, "Nice guys finish last...well it might as well be nice girls finish last, too".

We tell our story in the hopes that no one else might ever have to awaken to such a blustery snowy morning as we did.

Kristina Arielle Calco, forever and always the 'Good Girl', who dotted her "i's" with hearts and was blessed with the keen ability to see the absolute goodness in everyone.

You are the Rose About to Bloom

You are the rose about to bloom,
The color soon to wake,
The perfume set to scent the breeze,
The bud about to break.

You stand upon the lip of time
alight with what will be,
and see yourself out to the sky
across the open sea.

We see you vertically, a gift
too beautiful to plumb,
and treasure all the years you were
and all the years to come.

-by Nicholas Gordon (by permission)

*Given to Kristina on her 15th birthday, by her sister Gina,
nearly a full year before her death.*

Recipe for a Disaster:
Bullying to Depression to Suicide
By Kristina's mom, Michelle Calco

Every Waking Moment
I died a million deaths that cold December morning, and now, months later I die a little each day thinking about what went wrong in my precious young girl's life to cause her so much pain and suffering. Most days all I really feel like doing is crawling around on all fours. I often wonder if I can be excused from the rest of my life. I wonder if people would mind so very much if I were to just lay down in the middle of the supermarket and howl like a wild animal. I wonder if they'd excuse my behavior. I suppose it's not the proper thing do to, at least not in public, and so each day I literally force myself to carry on with life.

I am tormented by this terrible tragedy every waking moment, and even as I type these words, I ponder the fact that I never really understood what the words 'every waking moment' really meant. I'm absolutely certain a bereaved mother coined this phrase.

Each restless night I lay awake wondering and replaying my daughter's life, from beginning to end. Could there have been a way to change the outcome? How did things turn out like this? I punish myself over and over as do many like me. I yearn to have back those moments when I would complain about the mess that Kristina had made in the bathroom. In fact, I would give anything to find just one single strand of her hair on the bathroom floor.

I try my best to make sense out of the senselessness. I piece together the pieces of the puzzle and work towards enlightening people. I know this is what the 'good girl' whose deepest desire was 'to become a great scientist and help humanity in some way' would want, and so I try my best to honor her wishes.

Bullying: Nasty Words Can Kill
Sticks and stones may break my bones, but words can never hurt me...or can they?
Shortly after Kristina's death, our local elementary school hosted a Children's Science Fair. The students created colorful boards to display photos along with their stated Purpose; Hypothesis; Materials Used; Procedure; Variables and Conclusion.

Student projects ranged in topic from which liquid will preserve a cucumber the best to the effects words have on rice. Yes, you read that correctly. I thought that same thing. What does that mean? I paused, as I thought for sure I had read it incorrectly. To my surprise, this was actually a valid experiment in which the question was posed, "What did the power of words have on rice?" At first, I didn't quite understand what the experiment was all about... but as I read on, things became all too clear to me.

This experiment involved simple white rice, which was cooked and divided equally amongst 6 clean baby food jars. Two jars were simply set aside. The remaining four jars, had messages, which were taped on so that the words faced the rice.

On the first note, were the words "I Love You". On the second note, "I believe in you and have Faith in you". On the third note, "I hate you". On the final note, "You are sad and disgusting and you will never amount to anything".

These jars were set aside for a few weeks and closely observed.

Would you be surprised to know that the rice with the nasty words rotted and turned moldy and green? The rice that had no words deteriorated at a moderate level. The rice with the kind and loving words showed barely any deterioration at all. Truly amazing.

Do I need to tell you how this one simple experiment touched me? How perfectly and incomprehensibly it just happened to be there, catch my eye, and with creative precision, target the exact issue I was wrestling with.

And can you imagine, if negative words can turn a jar of pure white rice moldy and green, what those same words can do to a person?

It is estimated that approximately 90% of all suicides are a direct result of depression. Depression is caused by a chemical imbalance in the brain. Bullying is widely accepted as a depression trigger...anything that happens physically or emotionally that can cause an imbalance within the normal brain function. We can therefore confidently say that bullying can lead to depression by physically/chemically altering normal brain function.

This should be clear to you from the described rice experiment above. Isn't the oxidation and decay of the rice a physical/chemical process? And didn't we already show that this process is altered with the choice of words used to affect the rice? Simple words - effecting chemistry. If you were in my shoes, you would know it's true.

Depression and Suicide
So many people wonder WHY a person becomes depressed, as depression is such a very hard concept to understand, and certainly has different levels, manifestations, and ramifications. Why would a young person, who has everything to live for, suddenly and abruptly end his or her own life?

Kristina was suffering from depression, which unfortunately went unrecognized; I have learned a lot since Kristina's death...and would like to share some of that with you. Much of the following information is borrowed from one county's Suicide Prevention Program and has been interspersed with Kristina's personal information:

Brain Chemistry
You have learned in biology that our bodies are made up of cells. The brain and the spinal cord are made up of 300 billion special cells called neurons.

Neurons act like electrical wires. They send messages to all of our body parts to do something. Neurons tell our lungs to expand and contract so that we breathe. They tell our heart to beat, and they tell our intestines to process food into energy. They also tell our legs and arms to move.

Another function of neurons is to put together all of the information that we get from the world around us in order to create the way we look at life. We call this 'thinking'.

If the neurons are not working correctly, we won't function well. For example, if the spinal cord is injured, the electrical messages stop from the injury down and the body parts below the injury will not move anymore. If the neurons that cause us to think are not working correctly, our thought patterns change.

The problem is that this is a very tricky electrical system because no two neurons touch. There is actually a space between each one—a synapse. Our brains are an electrical system that has 300 billion 'shorts' in it. If we cut a lamp's electrical cord in half, the electric current stops running and the lamp won't work; similarly with the brain.

The electric current keeps flowing through the brain because we have natural chemicals (called neurotransmitters) that are between each neuron. These chemicals allow the 'electricity' to keep moving.

When there are not enough of these chemicals, the electric current is altered, or slows down. Our thinking changes too. This is what results in a condition known as a 'chemical imbalance'.

When we can't think as effectively as usual, we can't concentrate, it gets hard to problem solve, we start to feel badly about ourselves, we get frustrated and angry, and we feel sad and hopeless. All of these are symptoms of depression, rooted in brain chemistry.

It is very, very important to get help for people who are suffering from depression. Depression works on a continuum, and left untreated, it begins to affect more and more areas of the brain. Untreated depression is the number one cause of suicide. And suicidal thoughts often begin when depression reaches an advanced stage. You must remember, however, that suicide can be stopped at many points along the continuum. It regularly is in many cases. In others, unfortunately, it is not.

In Kristina's case, her brain patterns were not working properly. Her brain was *sick*. The brain is an organ of the body, and can get 'sick' just like the heart, liver and kidneys. Most normal people will seek medical attention for a broken arm; they would never attempt to fix the problem by themselves. Unfortunately, people do not often recognize the advancing continuum of depression and they tackle it at every stage, just as they did in the beginning, on their own. This is a mistake. And it's a dangerous one to make. Please seek help for depression and implore others to do so as well.

Kristina was hurting inside and all she really wanted was to feel better. She didn't know that if she got help, those feelings would go away. Depression can be treated and the bad feelings...those of hopelessness and worthlessness, can be eliminated.

Recipe for a disaster
This "recipe" is for you to ponder. It will help you follow the signs and dangers of bullying and its relationship to both depression and suicide. It will reveal the inner workings of a sweet and naïve young girl and the effects of varied external circumstances on those inner workings. Not everyone who is bullied will suffer from depression, and not everyone who suffers from depression will die by suicide. But certain children are clearly at a higher risk for serious bullying induced depression, and possibly, suicide. Kristina was one of these children. I have put together the following analysis, *Kristina's recipe*, to enlighten others on the risks they may face with their own children.

So what made Kristina different from many others who may have suffered similarly, but do not end up clinically depressed or suicidal?

Take one part shy & sensitive, impressionable, naïve young girl...
Take one part shy and sensitive, impressionable, naïve young girl and add a lack of self-esteem. Slowly stir in puberty. Add typical teenage pressures including friends, grades, sports, extracurricular activities and being perpetually on Instant Chat. Mix in what turns out to be a sexually charged and romantic online relationship with a boy from another high school. Add a daily dose of teasing, ridicule and torment by a group of boys and garnish with a seeming inability for intervention in any way, shape or form. Shake well and then let sit.

Here is a lovingly written letter, which we received shortly after Kristina's death. It conveys Kristina's unmistakable kind and generous personality:

"Kristina was such a wonderful person. I love everything about her. ...She always had everyone laughing and made you feel so good about yourself. ...She was so loving and never ever brought you down. ...no matter what I say or how much I write I could not come close to covering how amazing she truly was and is. ...She was a confident girl and could open up so easy to people. ...I remember that in elementary school we went rollerblading at "Great Skate" for her Birthday. We pretty much had the whole rink to ourselves. It was one of the best Birthday parties ever. ...She was always so giggly and had this innocence to her personality. ...Even though Kristina had such a short life, she accomplished so much including filling and touching the hearts of everyone she met. I really truly don't think Kristina wanted to upset any of us. She just was looking for a way out of whatever she was upset about and ended up making a huge mistake. She wasn't a selfish girl and I hope nobody will remember her like that. ...It's hard to associate suicide with Kristina because it wasn't her. At least on her last night she looked gorgeous. ...I told her I would have been sad if she hadn't come and she looked so, so pretty she said 'awww really?' and 'thank you'. Before I left, she gave me the biggest hug I have ever had. That night Kristina never stopped smiling. ...I will always remember that smiling Kristina and miss her always and forever. She has touched me in many ways. She is probably smiling down on us with her beautiful smile watching us. Kristina wasn't just a 4-point-0, a memory, a friend, a daughter, a sister, or a story. She has now become part of my heart and I'm sure she's part of yours and many others."
--A friend

Add a lack of self-esteem...

"Am I pretty?" "Sometimes I think I am and sometimes way not...Am I fat? Yes. That's why I've been running, but I need to run more & eat less."

This is a direct quote from one of Kristina's 7th grade journal entries. Seems like a very typical sentence from any 13-year-old girl. Contrast that one to one found in her 10th grade journal:

"Am I ugly? Guess so...every time I look in the mirror & think I look just a little cute or pretty, I instantly yell at myself & say 'no ur not pretty at all...ur really, really ugly."

One friend wrote about what Kristina had to endure in middle school:

"I had a friend named Kristina Calco who throughout middle school was bullied, bossed around, made fun of and embarrassed on a daily basis at school and totally tormented. She was Beautiful... my group of friends and I loved her for who she was. She could never be mean to anyone. She NEVER talked about anybody behind their backs. People told her she was ugly, fat, stupid, and she was told she could never be with anybody in a relationship. Let me tell you, this beautiful girl, not ugly, not fat, was probably around 110 pounds in middle school. She wasn't stupid. She had straight A's. She had pranks pulled on her all the time... she'd cry in the bathroom and I'd hold her in the hallway when someone said something mean to hurt her."

Is it any wonder how a young girls' self-esteem could be changed by remarks from a group of boys? Because of the type of person that Kristina was, she was greatly impacted by the bullies. While it may seem quite simple for you or me to have told the bullies to get lost, Kristina simply could not do this. She wasn't that type of person. Instead, she tried to befriend them. One year, she went so far as to send a couple of them Christmas cards. When one boy emailed her as to why she would do such a thing; why, didn't she hate him? She responded that she didn't hate him, that she just thought he wasn't very nice sometimes. In her journal, she wrote, "I think I've just made a couple of boys' days. It feels good to be nice."

Slowly stir in puberty...
I have heard it said that puberty in and of itself can be a form of mental illness. So many changes are happening at the chemical level. To go through puberty without being bullied is hard enough, but when you add bullying to the mix, the combined changes can form a lethal mix.

What I believe happened to Kristina is that at the time that she was being bullied, she also began her journey through puberty. I truly believe that the combination of the two was just too much for Kristina, given the type of person that she was, and she ultimately began to suffer from depression.

I can honestly say that something about Kristina changed in the middle of the 7th grade. Kristina became angry all the time at home. She took her aggressions out on everything and anyone. Although this is typical behavior for a bullied child, we did not know at this time that Kristina was being bullied. We were at a complete loss to explain her behavior and when we questioned her, she too could not explain her behavior. We ended up chalking her behavior up to typical teenage adolescence. Unfortunately, we were wrong.

Add typical teenage pressures...
As we all know, being a teenager is hard enough. But in these modern times, even more pressure abounds. Not only is there pressure to perform well academically, but today's youth are also pressured to perform well in sports, become involved in extracurricular activities, and generally fit in. Add to this the ever-increasing pressure to look thin and beautiful, created not only by the mass media, but by society as a whole, and the result is a plethora of complications ranging from eating disorders, body dimorphic disorder, dieting, cosmetic and plastic surgery, to depression and suicide. If you think that covers everything, well, we can't forget to include the impact of technology. Everything from cell phones to AIM (Instant Messaging), and social network websites are now serving to further complicate the lives of the average young adult.

Have you ever considered the power of personal space? Have you ever noticed that people are much less apt to be rude the closer in proximity that they are? It is much more likely that you will experience 'road rage' than 'supermarket rage'. People have a certain comfort level based on distance. This is why when you ride on an elevator, no one speaks. The personal space is just too close. The more distance, the more you open up.

This concept can similarly be transferred over and applied to the Internet. The Internet is so unlike many other forms of communication. It's unlike the phone in that there are no tonal interpretations or verbal cues, such as inflections in voice. It's unlike personal contact in that there are no facial expressions to interpret, nor is there any body language to interpret. The Internet is an entirely different type of animal, and as such, it is one that we as parents are not familiar with, especially where its implications for our children are concerned.

The slang language of the Internet, such as, "lol", "g2g", "ttyl", is an entirely different form of communication. In _Girl in the Mirror_, Dr. Ilene Berson of the University of South Florida was interviewed and expounds in detail on much of what I have already stated. Additionally, she claims that the inherent capability of the Internet allows for experimental behavior not ordinarily to everyday behavior by its users. So what does this mean to you and me? Well, the implications are that your children are doing and saying things that would absolutely knock your socks off if you knew. Believe me, if you knew what I know now, you might change the way you view your child's activity on social network websites and the various Instant Messengers.

Dr. Berson writes that, "Girls using the Internet sometimes don't see themselves as communicating with the 'real' world, but see it as a game which is permitting them to explore different things about themselves." Berson further theorizes, "Some girls use the Internet to explore negative behaviors such as having sexually suggestive chats". Further, she states that the girls who are using the Internet in ways that are negative are almost universally unsupervised, and tend to be the ones who are online for an extensive period of time. This increases the likelihood of negative interactions and 'risk-taking'. Berson poses the societal questions, "Is it okay to be engaging in these online fantasies?", "How will they (the chats) affect these girls' social and emotional development?" and "How will the nature of communication on this new medium affect our children?"

Back in 2003, I allowed Kristina to download AOL instant messenger. She was 13 years old and in the 8th grade. She told me that 'everyone else was using it', and so I agreed. Although our computer is in the middle of our home, I let my daughter have free reign to use it at will. She spent an inordinate amount of time at the computer and although it did concern me, I allowed her to continue, as it seemed to be one of the few things that really made her happy. I could never have imagined the power that I was handing over to a 13-year-old girl.

Mix in what turns out to be a sexually charged and romantic online relationship with a boy...
When she was just 15 years old, BEFORE KRISTINA ENTERED THE 10TH GRADE, my daughter started dating a 15-year-old boy who she met on the Internet. He was a friend of a friend. Although they only saw each other in person about a dozen times, they chatted and emailed each other numerous times daily over the course of approximately 3 months. IT SEEMED LIKE INSTANT CHEMISTRY AND THEY SOON BECAME boyfriend and girlfriend.

Kristina could not believe that she finally had a boyfriend. She couldn't believe that someone really liked her and thought that she was beautiful. What a change for Kristina. She emailed to him, that, "No one had ever been so nice to her before, at least not a boy". Through 2 1/2 months of emails, Kristina was now being told how absolutely gorgeous, hot and sexy she was. In Kristina's eyes, this was true love. They told each other that they would be together forever and being the young naïve girl that she was, Kristina began to trust every word that was said to her. In the few times that they actually saw each other in person, Kristina fell head over heels in love. As the emails became increasingly sexual in nature and Kristina began to allude to her receptivity to more than a friendly kiss. However, Kristina's morals were deeply ingrained and ultimately she could not in her heart of hearts back up her promises. When Kristina wasn't able to follow through, the relationship was ended via, of all things, an instant message. Kristina was absolutely shattered. She fell into a tailspin beyond which there seems to have been no redemption.

It soon became apparent to Kristina that the entire relationship had been based on sex and not love. Kristina soon began to rationalize that everything that had come out of this relationship was a lie, which meant that she wasn't beautiful, gorgeous, or sexy or any of those wonderful things she had been told that she was. Like many young girls, Kristina had followed her heart instead of her head, and now her entire world was beginning to collapse. Once again, Kristina, unable to make sense of this relationship that had spun so madly out of control, went back to the notion that she was unworthy of being loved. She went back to the banter of the bullies. Instead of seeking help for her pain, she turned it inwards on herself and became her own worst enemy. She was the ugly, nasty one after all, and she simply didn't deserve to live.

Based on Dr. Berson's interview, one can easily fit the pieces together to figure out what happened next. The girl who wore the 'I'm worth waiting for' pin, which she'd received from Teen Heart, could never live up to her Internet 'fantasy' life, and in the end, the 2 ½ month long relationship was abruptly ended via an instant message. That was on or about November 3, 2005. On December 4, 2005, after a late night and into the morning online instant message conversation with her ex-boyfriend, my 15-year-old daughter, Kristina Calco, took her life by suicide.

Add a daily dose of teasing, ridicule and torment by a group of boys...
Somewhere in the middle of the 7th grade, Kristina began to be picked on at school by a group of boys who called her 'ugly and nasty' on a daily basis. She endured this for approximately 2 1/2 years. Her friends say that she cried in the cafeteria or the bathroom every day. The type of bullying

that Kristina suffered is termed emotional bullying. It can include such things as tormenting, ridicule and humiliation. Kristina's friends did not have a clear understanding of the definition of bullying and they thought that they were doing the right thing by consoling Kristina every day. They didn't understand how persistent bullying could induce depression, low self-esteem, shyness, poor academic achievement, isolation or suicidal thoughts.

As such, neither Kristina, nor any of her friends ever told on the bullies.

Garnish with a seeming inability for intervention in any way, shape or form...
Suicide is the third leading cause of death among young people ages 15-24 yet despite having access to the *Youth Suicide Prevention School Based Guide*, (YSPSBG), many school districts have been reticent in adopting effective evidence based programs and have either no plan or partial plans for suicide prevention in effect.

Just for curiosity's sake, let us look at an absolute worst-case scenario of what could happen, when a school district casts aside YSPSBG guidelines, and chooses to follow its own guidelines instead. If you'll bear with me, I think you'll see the relevance when we reach the end of the discussion.

Imagine a well-respected school district, which for all intents and purposes appears to be following a very well intentioned suicide prevention program, but has no system in place for training its staff, or for parent involvement and notification.

Next, let's take an honor student from high school who begins to confide in one of her parents that she has a recent inability to comprehend her reading material, focus; and that it seems to "take an hour to read a single page"; she can no longer concentrate on her studies. She begins to think that perhaps she has ADD or Dyslexia.

Since there has been no parent information sent out, and knowing absolutely nothing about adolescent depression, the parent of this student might believe that her child simply has too much on her plate. Soon, and out of the ordinary, the child begins to stay up late into the night to complete her studies. It is at this point that the parent turns to the only place that makes sense for him or her to ask for help, the school.

One day this parent drives in off the street, with no appointment, to speak to the Assistant Principal. It seems clear to her that at the very least maybe her child needs to be taken out of her honors classes.

After speaking at length with the Assistant Principal, the parent is told that the Guidance Counselor would be informed and to expect contact soon. When the Guidance Counselor calls, the parent reiterates all of her concerns. The parent is told that all of the child's teachers will be contacted to see how the child is doing.

When the Guidance Counselor calls again, she conveys that the child is maintaining her 4.0 status and that there are no immediate concerns from any of the teachers. Keep in mind that there has been no formal staff training on depression/suicide. As such, no one is able to recognize the 'recent and pronounced inability to concentrate', as being one of the primary signs of potential suicide in an adolescent.

At this time, a memo is distributed amongst the teachers instructing them to 'lighten up' on this child. Additionally, the Guidance Counselor calls the child in to see how she is doing, at which time the child manages to convey that she is 'doing great'.

The school's reaction is not very comforting to the parent who now calls the Administration Building and speaks to the Assistant Superintendent who proceeds to tell her 'not to worry', that 'we will definitely get to the bottom of things', and that 'someone will be getting back to you with some answers'.

The Guidance Counselor calls back once again insistent that from her vantage point nothing looks out of the ordinary. Unfortunately, without having had the appropriate training, the counselor is at a loss to properly identify a clear sign of potential suicide in an adolescent, and the warning signs clearly indicated by the parent.

Within a matter of days, things escalate and the absolute worst thing imaginable occurs. The child commits suicide.

It is at this point that I wish I could say that none of this ever really took place, but unfortunately, this is not fiction. This was what happened in Kristina's case.

When I look back at things now, it seems so unreal that no one thought it out of the ordinary that a parent of a 4.0 honor student with no prior history of problems might drive in off the street looking for help. Not one person was familiar with the signs of potential suicide in an adolescent, including myself.

As a final blow, shortly after Kristina's death, we discovered that back in May 2005; one Ninth Grade class at Kristina's school was not quite ready for the 4 day long intensive Gatekeepers Depression/Suicide Awareness training. Evidently, this class had fallen behind in their curriculum and so 'didn't have the necessary time'. As a result, their teacher cancelled the training. Unfortunately, this was Kristina's class.

On July 20th, 2006, a new Michigan Law, (HB 4375), was enacted which backs the efforts of the YSPSBG by 'encouraging' the board of a school district to provide age-appropriate information, as well as professional development for school personnel, concerning the warning signs and risk factors for suicide and depression and the protective factors that help prevent suicide. This new law further calls for those school districts providing such instruction to notify parents on the instructions being provided.

Ours has been a true tragedy in every sense of the word, a real life 'series of unfortunate events', a *recipe* for disaster, if you will. Even with this tragedy and the enactment of a state law 'encouraging' action, will things change? What will it take to 'encourage' school districts to adopt effective evidence based suicide prevention programs? Perhaps knowing the details of what happened to an innocent 15-year-old girl can impart on at least one community a sense of how critical it is to find out.

Shake well and then let sit
IN THE LAST FEW WEEKS OF KRISTINA'S LIFE, SHE WAS DEALT MANY BLOWS, WHICH INCLUDED, BUT WERE NOT LIMITED TO NOT MAKING THE VARSITY CHEERLEADING SQUAD, BECOMING ESTRANGED FROM HER FRIENDS, ENDING A RELATIONSHIP WITH HER VERY FIRST BOYFRIEND, AND NOT MAKING THE VOLLEYBALL TEAM. Nearly a month after the breakup, when Kristina returned home from the dance that fateful winter night, she got online and began an Instant Message Conversation with her ex-boyfriend that lasted into the early morning hours. After their online conversation, Kristina got up from what she was doing and walked out of everyone's lives for good. She left the computer on, her I-pod plugged in, her homework on the floor and her room a mess.

Sometime after 2am, on Dec. 4, 2005, Kristina made her way downstairs, shut off the lights and hung herself. She died in the same manner that she described herself in her diary.....feeling ugly, sad, alone, and hurt.

Bullying is a very real issue
During the course of our busy days and lives, we often do not think about the impact that our words or our actions have on one another, especially

one as sensitive as Kristina. Know that every word, deed, thought, action and intention can and does potentially touch thousands of other lives.

But there is much more to be learned here - REMEMBER KRISTINA. That's the name of a group that a friend of Kristina's started on Myspace.com. Despite the things that happened to Kristina, she remained a genuinely kind and loving girl who made an outward effort to be nice to everyone.

In Kristina's case, the bullies truly changed the course of Kristina's life, which in turn affected many other lives, including all of those who read these words, and hear Kristina's story. We each have the choice to be the kind of person that Kristina was: caring, kind, loving, generous and a friend to all. Kristina was a good natured, compassionate, kind-hearted, empathetic, loving girl who personified what 'unconditional love' truly is. That's the real lesson.

In Loving Memory

Kristina Calco
12/25/89 – 12/04/05
We all love and miss you more than words can say.
We'll see you again in Heaven.
And no, no one will ever forget you.

Love,
From Everyone You Ever Knew

[1]*AMERICAN FOUNDATION FOR SUICIDE PREVENTION (AFSP)*
http://www.afsp.org/index.cfm?fuseaction=home.viewPage&page_id=050FEA9F-B064-4092-B1135C3A70DE1FDA

[2]*SCHOOL-BASED YOUTH SUICIDE PREVENTION GUIDE -*
http://theguide.fmhi.usf.edu/

Death by Computer

*"A bully doesn't have to be eye to eye to bully someone.
Sometimes he or she gets into cyberspace, and then there's
no place to hide from their torment."*

Jeffrey's Story
Sixth out of Seven, Number-One Son, Right-hand Man

In loving memory of Jeffrey Scott Johnston - 12/21/89 – 6/29/05
By Debra Johnston

WHO AM I?
(In Jeff's Words)

I'm number six in a line of seven. I'm William's big brother and my Dad's number-one son. I'm uncle to Alex, Danny, and Amanda, and my mother's right-hand man. I'm the one the Admiral teachers depend on to bring their mail every afternoon, staple papers, and alphabetize emergency cards. I'm Mrs. Miller's moving crew, Dr. Miller's tic-tac fetcher, Mrs. Harmon's computer-booter, and Coach Henderson's improvement goal for the past semester. I'm a loyal friend, and a good secret-keeper. Sometimes, it's easier to describe who we are by examining what we mean to the people around us.

On the surface, there's nothing really special about my life so far. I was born at Cape Coral Community Hospital on Dec. 21, 1989. I lived in the same house until I was 10, before moving to a new house only five miles away. Although I never moved from Cape Coral, I have traveled to many places. I have been to fifteen states, and three countries. I've walked beside a volcano, climbed up waterfalls, and watched my mother gamble away my college funds in Las Vegas.

I'm not always traveling. In fact, my life is pretty routine. I wake up and go to school. Then I come home and do my homework while watching television. After that, I play video games until it's time for dinner. Finally, I go on the Internet until I get tired, and then I go to bed.

When I'm bored I like to build models as a hobby. I especially love building Zoid models because they are very detailed and very different from any other models. I also love collecting coins and cards. Another way I spend some free time is by shooting soda cans with my Red Rider BB gun. Most of the time, I just play video games.
Overall, I'm just a normal kid with a great life. I have a big family with caring brothers and loving sisters. My school is great, and my teachers are wonderful. I'm important to

other people, and I have big plans for the future. Even though I sometimes get frustrated, I always try to keep a big smile on my face.

In my future, I hope that I will get a scholarship to Harvard. I want to become a lawyer like my cousin Bobby, my grandmother and my great-grandfather. I guess I just have a knack for debating with people and solving things.

I come from a long line of lawyers. My cousin Bobby recently had a case in which he was on the news for. My great-grandfather was a great lawyer who participated in many well-known cases in Tennessee.

There are some other reasons why I want to become a lawyer. One reason is that lawyers make lots of money. Another reason I want to become a lawyer is so that I can debate with people all day long.

This passage was taken directly from the book written by Jeff about his life in the fall of 2002, shortly after beginning seventh grade. It was a project for a language arts class, where the bullying would later begin. On the cover was a collage of smiling faces, but you did not have to look hard to find Jeff there among his friends with his trademark grin stretching from ear-to-ear.

Jeff's words say far more about him than I could possibly describe, except to say that he was an "old soul" in a young body. Before starting school, Jeff spent his days hanging out with one or the other of his doting grandmothers. From my husband's mother, he developed a passion for animals and the desire to know all there was to know about them. From my mother, Jeff learned to love the law and a strong sense of right and wrong. She instilled in Jeff a belief in the value of truth, honor and justice. There is no doubt that the influence of these two, helped shape the character of our little man.

Jeff was a regular around the pool at my mother's condominium from the time he could toddle, and he spent his days conversing with his "friends" about their lives before retirement, the economy, politics and the weather. He was everyone's darling. His opinions were respected. His observations were validated. By the time he was ready for kindergarten, Jeff was a self-confident, yet humble charmer, who could start up a conversation with anyone. Jeff loved the world, and the world loved him! Then, in seventh grade, Jeff's world began to fall apart.

It started out the way most young love does, with a giggly girl and a boy that suddenly finds he is "going out," though in middle school that doesn't mean that you actually "go anywhere," just that you have a girlfriend the other guys will envy at school. Like most first relationships, Jeff was over-the-moon when it started and broken-hearted when it ended a few days later.

What upset him most was not that she had broken up with him, but that she refused to speak to him or tell him why. I comforted him as best I could, and went to bed with the confidence that young hearts heal quickly.

If you had asked Jeff to describe himself, he would have replied happily, as he did in his book, that he was "the sixth out of seven kids, his father's number one son, and his mother's right-hand man." He took great joy in the novelty of being from such a big family, and for eleven years, he basked in the glory of being the baby of the family.

From an early age, Jeff relished his role as "date bait" for his brothers. With his precocious wit and winning smile, he would capture the girl's heart, and then introduce her to his brother with an air of innocence worthy of an Academy Award. Jeff excelled in academics, and read everything he could lay his hands on. This combined with a vivid imagination, made Jeff an exceptional storyteller. The tree in our backyard might be a pirate ship one day, and a mystical castle the next, as Jeff would weave elaborate plots for the neighborhood kids to act out. He was a natural leader — outgoing and popular, loved by everyone.

One of Jeff's teachers compared him to one of the Japanese puzzles that he so adored. The pieces themselves were very simple. The fascination lay in the way they fit together. He was honest, sincere, sensitive, loyal, clever and kind. He was also stubborn, proud, disorganized and never above blackmail or a little loan-sharking when the opportunity presented him with the chance to outdo an older sibling. He would tease his little brother mercilessly, but spent endless hours playing with William, and would have defended him with his life.

Jeff loved to sing, but couldn't carry a tune. He could do ten things at once on a keyboard, but couldn't dribble a basketball. He conquered Honors Algebra II, but couldn't live with the fact that sometimes in life, there is no justice.

I can close my eyes, and I can still remember the excitement in his eyes when he told me that he was "going out" with the most beautiful girl in seventh grade.

As a middle school teacher, I was familiar with the heartache of young love and the speed at which seventh grade girls change their affections. I reassured him that it wasn't the end of the world, and that he would point to her picture in later years and wonder what he ever saw in her. I said it was nothing that a dish of ice cream couldn't cure. I close my eyes now and picture her, blonde-haired and dimpled ... chatty. I know her first name, but if I ever knew her last name – I have long since forgotten it. I've heard it said that something as simple as a butterfly fluttering its wings in Argentina could affect the weather in Europe. This is the idea, the moment I replay in my mind through long nights when sleep will not come. I ask myself what I might have done differently. For this was the beginning of the end.

I found Jeff in my classroom after school the next day. He was sobbing, and I knew that the pressure of holding all this in all day had cost him dearly. Now, the tears streamed down his face, and his shoulders shook with sobs. Finally, I was able to put the disjointed ramblings together enough to understand that he was still dealing with the backlash of his breakup. Now, however, it was not just a girl giving Jeff the silent treatment.

Several of the students who made up her circle of friends were whispering about him, and passing notes in class. It felt like everyone was in on the joke except him because, of course, HE was the joke they were sharing.

For the first time in his life, Jeff was isolated and alone. He tried to talk about what was happening, but the friends he held so dear all seemed to be rushing off on vague emergencies. Suddenly nobody had time to take his telephone calls. Nobody needed help on an assignment. Nobody felt like getting together - nobody, except Jeff.

The telephone calls began shortly after that. First came, an increase in the number of hang-ups. Then Jeff's almost frantic desperation was to answer it before anyone else picked up the phone. The tension became almost visible each time the phone rang, and Jeff would disappear behind a locked door. I could not hear the words, just the cadence of Jeff's voice. Sometimes he sounded angry, and others, almost pleading. I told myself he was growing up and needed to work out things for himself. However that was not sufficient to stop me from picking up the telephone to find out what was going on. On the other end, I heard HIS voice for the first time — the one that Jeff would come to refer to in his writing as "The Evil One!"

The voice on the phone said my son was a stalker, that everyone hated him, that he better stay away from Tiffany*. He said that she had never cared about Jeff and she was just playing with him. She and the others had all been laughing at how pathetic Jeff acted after the break-up. I imagined Jeff's face as he listened downstairs. I knew that the humiliation he felt at this diatribe was a thousand times worse by knowing that I was hearing it too. (*not her real name)

The calm that had been so carefully cultivated by years of teaching deserted me. The voice that responded to this verbal assault on my child was barely recognizable to me, but firm in the resolve to report this incident at school the following morning. There was no doubt in my mind that this would put a swift end to the harassment.

Perhaps the greatest irony of the events that followed over the next two years is that they were so faithfully and honestly documented, not by Jeff, the school or me — but by the bully himself.

In an open journal, the bully recorded the details of each milestone in his mission to demean and dehumanize Jeff. Like the serial killer that is compelled to taunt and goad the authorities with the details of his crime, the bully brazenly published what he was doing on his website. No effort was made to conceal his identity. "The Evil One's" work was done on his family's computer, and each entry signed with his name. I shudder to think of Jeff reliving the horror again and again, punctuated with the computer-speak epithet of "lol" (laughing out loud), that has become this generation's trademark shorthand textual phrase for humor, and, contemptuous scorn.

At this point, I am invariably asked why Jeff, or anyone for that matter, would bother to read the rantings of a person that admittedly considered most of his peers as inferior, ugly and well deserving of his disdain. What is it about human nature that defies logic and demands that we open Pandora's Box in full knowledge that it will be our downfall? It is a question that requires a greater mind than mine. I only know that it is a temptation that is as old as Eve and the apple, and that most of us would rather know the truth, however painful, than remain blissfully ignorant while everyone snickers and whispers behind our back.

I cannot account for why none of the dozens of students that had access to this site ever reported it to an adult until after Jeff's death by suicide almost two years later, but this is the reality of all bullying. It is a shadowy thing that can only exist behind a wall of silence. It feeds in the dark reality of imagined helplessness.

With the keyboard as his weapon, the bully violated the sanctity of my home and murdered my child just as surely as if he had crawled through a broken window and choked the life from Jeff with his bare hands. It was not a death that was quick and merciful. It was carried out with lies, rumors and calculated cruelty portioned out day by day. With the precision of a gifted surgeon, the bully cut away at the friendships of a lifetime – a lifetime of fifteen precious years.

My dreams are haunted by the vision of my son's suffering, as all pride, all happiness; all joy was stripped away until all that was left was a pain so great that the only escape for Jeffrey was in death.

There is a stigma connected to suicide and an unspoken code that often prevents families from ever obtaining closure for the death of a loved one. There are always the questions that pierce the heart, no matter how tactfully posed. "Did you ever suspect?" "Was anything done?" "How could no one have known?" There are no easy answers and for some survivors, there are no answers at all.

In our culture, suicide is often viewed as an act of cowardice ... a death without honor. I cannot believe that Jeff lacked either courage or honor. Though he demonstrates no remorse for his actions, the bully readily admits that Jeff never retaliated in any way. There were times when I was so frustrated by my inability to protect him that I wished that Jeff would defend himself physically. There was no question that Jeff was the stronger of the two. Had Jeff chosen to engage the bully using the Internet, he was certainly more than capable of holding his own. I may be wrong, but I cannot accept that it was Jeff who acted without honor.

I pray that one day I will find forgiveness, not for Jeff, but for myself for failing to have the courage and the strength to face the system and demand that my child be protected. Each day I watched my husband, our family and Jeff's friends struggle to forgive themselves for all the actions we did not take.

There will always be an empty space in our lives and in our hearts. There is a shadow behind every smile as we imagine Jeff at the wheel of his first car, in a tuxedo at his junior prom, walking across the stage at his graduation

Our life is now measured not in what we have, but in memories of what will never be.

None of us can undo the mistakes of the past, but we can learn from them. This is my legacy to Jeff. In his death I have found my voice. If everyone believed they had a voice, imagine how loud the noise would be!

Debbie's postscripts... **I wish you all "Penny Wishes"**
On June 29th, 2007 we marked the second anniversary of the last day of Jeff's life. Last year, we decided to celebrate Jeff's time with us at his favorite spot in the world...the Japanese Garden at Epcot (Florida). We hid a special pebble and a tiny star from Jeff's collection beneath a boulder near the bridge where Jeff and William posed for a photo before tossing "penny wishes" into the waterfall from that same spot the year before, just a week before Jeff's death. We filled our pockets with pennies, and spent the day reliving all the happy times as we walked from park to park, distributing pennies as we went, and inviting everyone to join us in sending thousands of penny prayers toward Heaven. This made such an impression on our younger son, William, that he chose this as the subject of his first school project ever, the "HUNDRED DAY PROJECT." *(See below)*

I would ask that every person reading this postscript to find a special place and toss in a special "penny wish" and say a prayer that God will protect ALL his children in despair and see them safely through till morning. Whenever I see all the coins at the bottom of a fountain, all I can think about is how wonderful the world would be if we tossed out acts of kindness the same way we toss our loose change, and had the same faith in their ability to improve the world! There are so many people that need our prayers right now...our soldiers, the sick, the hungry, the homeless. What is really wonderful is that the money collected from fountains is donated to charity, so our coins really could be the answer to someone's prayer. That penny you toss in may be used to give a special wish to a dying child or relief to a neighbor that lost everything in a storm. I can't think of any way that Jeff's life could be celebrated than to know that the world might be a kinder place for having known him. I know he could never pass up an opportunity to make a "penny wish" and staunchly believed that it would make the world better.

ONE HUNDRED "PENNY WISHES" by William Johnston (written while in Kindergarten)
When we pass a place that has a fountain, we always throw in a penny and make a wish. At Disney World, my brother and I would always throw a penny in the fountain, and wish that we would come back again soon. This is my mom and I throwing pennies in the fountain, and all the wishes going to Heaven to tell my brother, Jeff, that we miss him.

Special Submissions

The New Wave - A Warning about Cyberbullying

By Adrianna Sgarlata, Bully Police Virginia

Photo: Adrianna at age 9

Technology has altered our lives, dramatically, over the last few years. According to iSafe, Inc., (Internet Safety Education) an estimated 77 million youth, ages five through seventeen, regularly use the Internet.

When I was in high school, we used the Internet to look up news articles, find definitions of words, and to look at a website for our favorite brands. Today, children of all ages, and even adults, are using the Internet as a means of everyday communication via emails, instant messages, blogs, etc. In fact, these new technologies have moved beyond "everyday communication"; they have become their own form of communication, unlike anything we have seen before.

The detached nature of these new forms of communication offer bullies the opportunity to spread their messages of hate far and wide, with unusual speed, and a sense of anonymity. When the use of these communication tools becomes harmful to the feelings of another person, this is called cyberbullying.

In its broadest sense, cyberbullying is bullying (i.e., repeated attacks of another with the intent to harm someone, physically, emotionally, socially, etc.) using an impersonal form of communication, namely, electronic communication. While the intent of all forms of bullying may be the same, the differentiating factor between bullying and cyberbullying lies in the medium used to convey the message. This includes computers, cell phones, and any other devices that transmit messages from one person to another.

ISafe, Inc. adds this to the definition: Cyber Bullying is verbal harassment that occurs during online activities. It can take many forms, including:

- A threatening email
- Nasty instant messaging session
- A threatening email
- Repeated notes sent to the cell phone
- A website set up to mock others
- "Borrowing" someone's online identity and pretending to be them while posting a message.
- Forwarding supposedly private messages, pictures, or video to others.

We have heard the saying: "Sticks and stones may break my bones, but names will never hurt me". Sadly, this old saying is untrue. Names can, and do hurt. I know, because I was bullied as a child. I am Adrianna Sgarlata, and as I write this chapter, I'm also Miss Virginia 2006. Since my first pageant three years ago, the primary goal of the appearances I have made has been to call attention to the need to teach our youth not to bully, but instead how to behave respectfully and value others. When cyberbullying occurs, the respect and value we have for others is ignored, and the effects are devastating.

Cyberbullies use the anonymity of electronic communications over the Internet, in chat rooms, and through Instant Messaging (IM) for purposes of intimidation, embarrassment, or exclusion. They can quickly and easily generate trouble for others by creating false situations that reflect badly on someone else, which usually leads to a devaluation of the person being targeted.

As an example, pictures can be obtained through personal profile pages in social networking websites and then posted on social networking pages to embarrass a victim.

In one Virginia school I visited, a sixth grader had created an online poll to select the ugliest girl in the school, with the whole school able to cast votes. Other instances have included false and embarrassing information posted and hit lists of the top 5 or 50 students and teachers to target.

Instant Messaging, (IM), is a particularly dangerous medium for electronic communication. In addition, kids have developed very sophisticated mechanisms to target their victims. Cyberbullies have been known to change their on-line identity by creating new screen names, posing as a good friend of the victim, then engaging in conversations, inducing the victim to share things they would only share with a best friend. Many kids learn the hard way that in cyberspace, anyone can "be" anyone. Similar tactics are being used by sexual predators to lure children into sexual encounters...and worse.

The Effects of Cyberbullying

For decades, bullying has been regarded as an inevitable part of growing up – something a victim should simply "tough out", often referred to as "child's play." It's anything but. Now we know that the advice parents often give their child, "just ignore it", is simply not effective. Bullying won't go away, and you can't try to "talk it out" with the other child – that's not how bullies think. Bullies are mini-terrorists, and just as you aren't going to negotiate with terrorists, you aren't going to be successful at negotiating with bullies, or cyberbullies – if you can even find out who they really are. You must first try to prevent it from occurring, and if that fails, and you or your child becomes the victim of a cyberbully, you MUST document it, report it, and then block it. If you are a bystander, teacher, or parent, you must confront cyberbullying head on.

One thing we mustn't do is to allow it to continue. Because we know that bullying is linked to depression, suicide, (the third leading cause of death among teenagers), vandalism, shoplifting, truancy, drug and alcohol use and violence. I believe that cyberbullying has done one critically important thing to all of these effects of traditional bullying – it has accelerated them. What might have occurred over months, to bully someone to death, literally, can now take place online, instantly, in hours, and certainly days. To be anything less than vigilant and alert to cyberbullying problems is to have careless disregard for the safety of your child. It is very real.

Acts of cyberbullying are more powerful than spoken words, because they have the ability to be heard by thousands, tens of thousands, even millions of others. A harmful or mocking video of your child, of anyone, can be posted online for an instant distribution, and your child becomes an instant star, or laughing stock to the masses. There is even a new type of planned cyberbullying called, "cyberbashing", where bullies videotape an assault on a chosen victim and then post it on various movie and cam-cording submission websites. Such videos have now been aired on national news and talk shows. Essentially, the victim is victimized over and over again, as comments are solicited about the "fight" and/or, how good the "beating" was, compared to other videos that have been posted.

Who's cyberbullying who?

The iSafe America research team has discovered a disturbing trend—cyber bullying has affected more than half the students surveyed. This is quite a jump from the 15% to 20% estimated to be victimized by physical bullying.

Their latest assessments surveyed more than 1500 students ranging from fourth to eighth grade across the country. They found out:

- 58% of kids admit someone has said mean or hurtful things to them online
- 53% of kids admit having said something mean or hurtful things to another online
- 42% of kids have been bullied while online.

Even worse, iSAFE found that 58-percent of kids have not told their parents or any adult about something mean or hurtful that had happened to them online.

The tradition of home as a refuge from bullies on the school playground is over. The Internet is a new playground, and there are no off hours. The popularity of instant messaging, email, web pages, and blogging means that kids are a target 24 hours a day, seven days a week.

It is time for teachers, school officials and parents to become aware of the rising trend of cyberbullying, cyberbashing and other online harassment incidents.

Prevention – try to avoid the cyberbully

Below are some strategies that parents and teachers need to ensure students are taught what I now refer to as the "4th R", RESPECT.

- Don't give out or post on social networking sites any private information such as passwords, pin numbers, name, address, phone number, school name, or family and friends' names. Bullies and other harmful people on the Internet can use this information. Don't ever reveal your password to your friends. They might reveal it or use it against you in a fight. This happened to my brother. It can, and will happen, if you are not careful.
- Don't exchange pictures or give out email addresses to people you meet on the internet. Ask permission from parents when it is necessary to give such information.
- Avoid adding strangers to either your buddy list or to your social

networking site. This is critical, and most children do not follow this advice.

- Don't send a message when you are angry—it's hard to undo things that are said in anger, especially online.
- Block messages from people you don't know, or those from people who seem intent on unhealthy dialogue. Do not engage them in conversation.
- When something doesn't seem right, it probably isn't. Get out of the site, chat, etc.
- Realize that online conversations are not private. Others can copy, print, and share what you have said or any pictures you have sent. Be careful! Expect *zero* privacy.

Action Steps when Prevention Isn't Working - What to do?
First and most importantly, DON'T fight back online – or the bully will be able to claim you "started it". The cyberbullying could go on and on and get worse and worse.

Next, tell a trusted adult, and keep telling them until action is taken.

Copy EVERYTHING - Save all emails or instant-message conversations. Install "DeadAIM," a component to the AOL Instant Messenger (AIM) application, which allows users to find, chat and record conversations between friends, as well as enemies.

Use tools like http://www.spectorsoft.com/ to monitor your child's internet use if you believe that they are being bullied, but will not speak up about it.

Set up a Google alert on your child's name, to be notified whenever anything is posted online with your child's name in it. I am notified daily on any postings with my name, Adrianna Sgarlata. Go to "Google," click on "News," than at the left "Google Alerts."

Parents, only use the services of an ISP with parental controls. Don't ask your child to set the parental controls up for you. That defeats the purpose of the controls. Be sure your child or children can't guess the password. Change it frequently if necessary.

The safest place to put a family computer is in the most used room of the home – the place where most of the family traffic is.

Warn your child about cyberbullying. This warning could be as crucial to their survival as telling them not to play in the street.

Learn how to check the "history" of your child's online activities. Computers store the history but computer savvy kids today usually know enough to clear it out before they finish their session. We all know that teenagers can get careless, eventually.

If your son or daughter is getting threatening email, your local police department may be able to help or lead you to a private investigator with computer skills. If the emails are terrorist type threats, report this immediately to the police, who will then report it to the F.B.I. Since Columbine, sharp students alerting authorities have thwarted several internet terrorist threats against schools.

Note that in all these instances, immediate ACTION is required. Don't wait for things to get worse.

Advice for Victims of Crimes
You ARE a victim of a crime if you are bullied physically and sexually. Federal laws protect every citizen, young or old, from assault. Your State law may also solidify your child's human rights if they have an anti bullying law. (See www.bullypolice.org).

You MAY BE a victim of a crime if you are cyberbullied. It will take a little more digging and research to determine your rights under state and federal laws. Many states are formulating cyberbullying laws right now.

With stalking laws, there is a "reasonable person standard" that state laws will often employ to determine if a crime has been committed – namely, would the cyberbullying cause alarm, annoy, or harass a reasonable person. If so, a crime is being committed. It's really going to be up, in large part, to YOU to make a claim.

Conclusion
After talking with kids, and working with numerous organizations like Bully Police USA and iSafe, Inc., I know for a fact that children and teens feel that bullying and cyberbullying, is not just a big problem, but perhaps the number one problem they face every day. In survey after survey, they see bullying as a bigger problem than peer pressure, drugs, drunk driving, cultural diversity, or the pressure of sexual promiscuity.

I lived through some harrowing bullying experiences and feel fortunate that it hadn't gotten bad enough to drive me to take my life, but all of us are wired differently. What is bearable to some may be unbearable to others.

Give yourself a daily 'check-up from the neck up'; these self tests apply to cyber communication as well as everyday conversations: Are you 'Behaving Respectfully and Valuing Others', and showing it in your actions and in the words you speak, to your spouse, your children, while driving, while chatting on the phone, while emailing others? Are you teaching these basic principles to others, including your children? Only if you actively work at this daily, can you truly become part of the solution and not part of the problem.

Judging the Methods of Suicide

By Jared's mom, Brenda High

I didn't want to write this chapter, but I believe it needs to be written. There will be those who will read these stories and almost certainly pass judgment on three of the mothers in this book based on one thing, the method of suicide our children chose.

In 2006, a computer game called, "Bully" was soon to be offered to the public. Believing this game had negative consequences for youth, Rochelle Sides, (Corinne's mother), started a campaign to fight its release.

It was unbelievable how many truly nasty people came forward to "bully" Rochelle because of her activism. And when I say nasty, I mean obscene and filthy in language, as well as cruel and mean in their personal comments towards her.

Somehow, the foul-mouthed cyber-attackers found out that Rochelle's daughter, Corinne, used a gun to take her life. This was all the information these individuals needed to begin their verbally abusive rampage.

I won't quote any of the profane emails, but I will quote one email that really hurt me; I'm sure Rochelle was hurt too...

"...I don't use the term mother, because a mom wouldn't expose her child to guns, she is the one who killed her own kid by having something like that in the house."

Somehow, motherhood (or parenthood) is in question if a child uses a gun as a method of taking their life. But what if a child uses a rope they found in the garage, poison found under the sink, a family member's prescription drugs found in the bathroom cabinet, a belt bought for a pair of jeans, a backpack strap bought for school, jumps off a local bridge or cliff, purposely drowns in the family swimming pool, stabs themselves in the chest with a knife or Samari Sword, uses the fumes of the family car to asphyxiate themselves, intentionally crashes into a pole or tree with the car daddy bought for him/her on their birthday, stole money from mom's purse and bought drugs to overdose on, or, what if the child stole a gun from a store and then took their life? Would the judgments be the same? What if the child stole the gun from a neighbor? Would the judgments be the same? These are all methods regularly used by young people to take their own lives.

It is never okay to judge if a mother is a good mother, or if parents are good parents, if a gun was used as a method of suicide. We should never judge. Instead, we should try to better understand the root emotional causes of suicide so we can help avoid these senseless tragedies in the future.

We have heard the questions - why was there a gun in the house? Why were you so careless? I can guarantee to all of you that no parent knowingly or willingly provides a suicidal child with any means to carry out the act of suicide. Many instruments such as guns, ropes, drugs and cars can easily be obtained or "borrowed" outside of the home. As for bridges, cliffs and pools, they are a part of the American landscape and accessible to all.

Ask yourself... does anyone really believe that their child is capable of killing themselves? I didn't believe my son was capable of it. We didn't know our son was depressed. He didn't tell us what he was planning to do, nor did we receive a suicide note. Yes, I do agree that parents who realize that their child is depressed and suicidal should remove weapons from their home. They should also remove medications, over-the-counter drugs, ropes, and not let the child drive. But, if a child truly wants to die, short of parents putting them into a mental institution, they will find a way. ...And mental institutions have even had suicides, as suicidal patients have hung themselves or jumped out of windows. If a person is determined to die it would be impossible to lock up every device, and deadly tool that can be used to take one's life. If you looked around the room you are sitting in right now you could easily see dozens of things that could be used to hurt or kill yourself.

Blaming a gun for a death, by suicide, school shooting, murder or any crime will not change anything in our society. Prevention doesn't come from analyzing the method of death, but from analyzing the root causes of death...do you kill a weed by cutting off the top of the leaves or do you go in and dig out the root?

According to "Leading Cause of Deaths Reports" from The Centers for Disease Control and Prevention, (www.cdc.gov), heart disease is the #1 way people die in the United States, with cancer coming in second. In addressing these causes, we see the end result and then look at ways to prevent that end result – better eating and exercising habits and good health and medical care. When suicide is the cause of death we need to look at ways to prevent that end result. We can do so by removing the factors that may cause depression (bullying, for example), which is the #1 root cause of suicide, and of course, providing good mental health care.

Bullying is only one of many triggers for depression. People who have traumatic events in their lives can easily develop depression. Bullying, divorce, death, car accident injuries, breaking up with a boyfriend or girlfriend, drugs, alcohol, developing cancer or any other disease, financial disasters (bankruptcy, losing a farm or home), the pressures from work or school/college, etc., are all major triggers to depression. (Be sure and read Summer Himes's chapter recounting her own depression and how debilitating depression can be).

We do not discount these other significant factors. However, where children are concerned, peer pressure, taunting, and bullying are often the root cause of real emotional distress, and depression. These things can lead to very serious consequences, including suicide. This is what *Bullycide in America* is all about, getting to the root of a BIG problem, an epidemic in today's societies, not just America, but all over the world – bullying.

"JUDGE not, that ye be not judged.

For with what judgment ye judge, ye shall be judged: and with what measure ye mete, it shall be measured to you again.

And why beholdest thou the mote that is in thy brother's eye, but considerest not the beam that is in thine own eye?

Or how wilt thou say to thy brother, Let me pull out the mote out of thine eye; and, behold, a beam is in thine own eye?

Thou hypocrite, first cast out the beam out of thine own eye; and then shalt thou see clearly to cast out the mote out of thy brother's eye."

Matthew: 7:1-5

Influences of the Media on Bullying

By Corinne's mom, Rochelle Sides

Thirty murders - Forty beatings. Does this sound like figures from a monthly or annual police report? Unfortunately, they are the number of violent acts a group of sixth-graders observed while watching *one hour* of prime-time television.

Television
According to several studies, children spend more time watching television than in any other activity except sleep. In fact the average American child will have watched 100,000 acts of televised violence, including 8,000 depictions of murder, by the time he or she is approximately 13 years old. *(Source: http://www.nsf.gov)*

The research found that youngsters who spent a typical amount of time - about 3½ hours daily, in front of 'the tube', had a 25 per cent increased risk of becoming bullies between the ages of 6 and 11.

As parents and members of a community, we constantly ask ourselves, how does TV and film affect our children? Would spending 3 ½ hours a day in front of 'the tube' increase the risk of our children becoming bullies or even becoming 'zombie' witnesses to others being bullied? Are children becoming desensitized to the pain, emotions and feelings of others because of what they are watching on television?

We know that TV has become increasingly more violent and graphic. How much has it increased? And what's the impact?

Studies conducted by UCLA have found that children may become 'immune' to the horror of violence; gradually accepting violence as a way to solve problems; imitating the violence they observe on television; and identifying with certain characters, victims and/or victimizers. This answers the question above desensitization. (www.ucla.edu)

Incidents of sexual violence and sadism doubled between 1989 and 1999, and the number of graphic depictions increased more than five-fold. (Source: PARENT TELEVISION COUNCIL, 1999)

Let's make some comparisons between TV 30 years ago in 1976, to 2006. In 1976, most families had one TV and three channels. We sat in the living room with our parents and watched shows like *Happy Days, Little*

House on the Prairie, The Walton's and if Dad was making the choice, *60 Minutes.*

These shows featured weekly situations that tested your favorite characters, and by the shows end provided a moral resolution that we could apply to our life, all the while making us laugh and cry. The characters were respectful to adults, the parents guided the children in the right direction, and their friends and family held them accountable when they did something wrong. If they lied or cheated, it was shown in a negative light.

In contrast, the homes today usually have a TV in the living room and in most bedrooms. The number one show in 2006 according to the Nielsen Ratings® is Desperate Housewives, a show that started the series with a suicide. It follows the love lives of divorced, married and single woman, and has issues ranging from alcoholism to adultery.

In 2001, a quarter of the most violent television shows, and two-fifths of the most violent movies, were rated R. The majority were rated PG or PG-13. (Source: CENTER FOR MEDIA AND PUBLIC AFFAIRS, 2001)

On average, children in the 23 countries surveyed watch television three hours each day, and spend 50 percent more time watching the small screen than they spend on any other activity outside of school. (Source: UNESCO, 1998)

Film
The top grossing movie of 1976 was *Rocky*, a story about a boxer that was down and out but with hard work, love and will power overcame his obstacles to become a champion.

In some of the recently released popular movie storylines:

• A murderer is glorified and on the FBI most wanted list
• A killer terrorizes a sorority house during the holiday season, and
• A teacher uses information about a colleague's private, illicit affair with a student to her advantage

Movie ratings are becoming less and less authentic, failing to give parents real direction on shows with inappropriate content. It used to be that a PG-13 rated movie could be trusted as safe with very little violence and sexual content and appealed to families, (consequently making more money than R-rated films). Now, you must wait until the "friend-reviews" come in before taking your family out to the movies.

It is common knowledge that the film industry has experienced a "ratings creep" where shows once rated R are now being rated as PG-13, in order to increase box-office profits and rental sales.

There is some oversight of who watches what in movie theatres. However, at home, it is an entirely different matter, there is little to stop minors from watching an R rated movie on TV or DVD/video. Minors can also order R rated (and sometimes X rated) movies on demand without a parent's permission...until the bill comes. The only true controls are diligent parents who have taken control of the television. Industry regulation and oversight is negligible.

Music
Songs in the Top 40 in 1976 were *Silly Love Songs* – Wings; *Don't go Breakin My Heart* – Elton John/Kiki Dee; *Disco Lady* – Johnnie Taylor; *December 1963* – Four Seasons; *Play That Funky Music* – Wild Cherry; all stories of love, broken hearts and melancholy.

The top 10 songs in today's world would have lyrics referencing convicts, strip bars, sex, drugs and prostitution. They are filled with profanity in almost every verse; they degrade women as a sexual object with no value.

Video Games
Currently we have video games with titles like *Grand Theft Auto*, *Bully*, *Resident Evil 4* and *True Crime: Streets of LA*.

Physical and sexual violence are commonplace in the video game industry. In some of the most popular games, the premise is for players to engage in violent criminal acts while earning points for attacking and killing innocent victims. Even with the M rating, for mature audiences, they are especially popular among pre-teens and teenage boys, who coincidentally, are in the first stages of forming relationships with women and girls.

This medium is perhaps the most dangerous of all. It has evolved quickly; regulation has always been slow to catch up, and behind the curve. It also actively engages children in violent acts, making the child just one step closer to acting the violence out in real life. And as mentioned, it has some very gender specific effects.

The top selling video games in 1976 were *Pong* and *Night Driver*, in contrast to today; these games were a test of simple skills, with very little moral implication. How long could you go without missing the Pong and how far could you drive at night without wrecking? Today's games are fraught with moral overtones and complicated emotional and physical themes. One could argue that they are *creating* a new reality for our children.

Positive Effects of Media

I don't want to mislead you into thinking that you need to remove every TV, stereo, DVD player, and game from your home; the media has positive effects as well.

For instance, several **news channels** have brought to light the disturbing trend of bullying and its effects, empowering parents and the community to fight for anti bullying laws, resulting in change at the schools our children attend.

Bully Police USA has a strong positive relationship with the news media, using it as a global tool to bring awareness to bullying and its victims and help lawmakers in every state understand the importance of good common sense anti bullying laws. Other such groups exist all over the country, positively impacting the media with messages and images.

There are also many **educational channels** on cable/satellite with quality viewing. Some of these are the Discovery Channel, the History Channel, FAM (Family Channel) and Disney Channels, religious programming channels, and self-improvement channels. There are some great family choices, with the keyword being "family" because how programming affects the family unit should be of the highest concern for parents...we just seem to have forgotten that as a society.

Now that we have the facts, and have opened a dialogue, what can we do to correct the problem? To make changes. First, it can be as simple as turning the channel on the TV when it becomes unsuitable. Change the radio station when it is offensive, and finally don't buy video games that promote physical and sexual violence. But, before that, it is most important to sit down as a family and decide what the family rules are, what is acceptable to listen to, view or play. Decide how much time will be spent on these activities. Make this issue a priority in your home. Talk about it at home. And follow through on your convictions. Do not let the media influence your children's morals and character, and shape who they are becoming. That is your job.

Shame and Blame:
The Code of Silence

By Tina's mom, Judy Kuczynski

Photo: Tina Kuczynski

Tina was a pretty, outgoing, friendly high school sophomore. In junior high she had been in the "popular" group but in high school she was the target of abuse and humiliation. Every day she found a different threatening note on her locker. The day I saw it, it said "Die Bitch!"

Old friends would call her up and pretend to want to make amends. The next day they would announce at school how pitiful she was and what she had told them in confidence over the phone.

The junior-senior prom that spring ended in disaster when a group of older girls surrounded her in the girls' restroom and spit on her and her silver prom dress.

That summer a group of boys put a bomb in the family mail box. It exploded and narrowly missed blinding her father when he went in to get the mail.

The incident that finally convinced Tina to leave that school was when a female classmate and a girl Tina did not know came to the place Tina worked and physically attacked her, accusing her of having said something to some guy Tina did not know.

It is difficult to understand or explain the dynamics of the effects such things, and this situation in general, had on the rest of us, Tina's family. As parents who tried to advocate for our daughter it was devastating to find no support from the school, from other adults, or from the healthcare establishment. No one had any answers or solutions. Our attempts made her an even bigger target. It got so bad that some classmates told her she would be killed if she didn't move.

Tina became deeply depressed and developed physical symptoms including chronic insomnia and TMJ so severe that she couldn't talk. She frequently asked why her friends hated her so much and what made her such an object of ridicule. I couldn't explain it to her. I couldn't fix it.

And I couldn't give her what she needed to be able to not care and get on with her life without these old "friends."

Tina wasn't the only one to develop physical symptoms. I also became clinically depressed. We both were put on antidepressants and went into counseling. I worried that she would try to hurt herself in an attempt to make the pain stop even though she never said she would do so.

Tina left that school before Christmas of her junior year and went to the local community college instead. Tina was 16. A year later, when she would have been a senior in high school, she was killed in a car accident. Many of her old crowd expressed sadness over not being able to explain to her why they had turned on her as they had. At her funeral, a number of them said that they had not been able to tell her they were sorry and they couldn't explain why they had not. To this day, even the bullies do not fully understand why they treated her with contempt. I certainly would like to understand it.

After Tina's death, I went back to school to earn a master's degree in professional counseling. As a registered nurse, I already knew something about the connection between depression and trauma but I needed to understand, to figure it out.

I found out that in adolescent peer groups there is overwhelming pressure to keep adults out. Peer aggression takes place in the social environment wherever children gather. It has always been difficult to spot because these behaviors are covert and for the most part practiced in a kind of secret code. As children grow older, they become more sophisticated in the covert techniques they use to abuse and hurt each other even while adults look on. When adults ask some adolescents outright about things they have seen, adolescents are reluctant to be honest. Their peer group has a great deal of power, power to make life miserable and at times impossible.

I found out that unwritten codes of conduct in our culture, such as the old saying about "sticks and stones," influence many American attitudes and behavior. One of the more powerful unwritten codes is a code of silence. The code of silence is a problem in most Westernized countries.

According to Dr. Dan Olweus, the renowned expert on peer abuse, the bully, the victim, and any witnesses remain silent because of a stigma in our society against telling tales. Adults don't want to encourage tattling and believe that the behavior that is being reported is insignificant. Children don't want to be hated by their friends or classmates because they have been unfaithful to the group by revealing behavior that could get one of them into trouble.

A code of silence is also part of the protective boundaries established and enforced by peer groups, gangs and families. This can be seen as a major influence in the dynamics of domestic abuse. Group members (family members) are censored and threatened for violating the secrets of the inner workings of the group (family).

Isolation is an especially effective and subtle tool to ensure that group members comply and keep the secrecy of the inner workings of the group. It is extremely powerful against adolescents who need to belong, to be reassured of their place in a community of their peers and their value to it. Isolation keeps outsiders out and it binds members in loyalty to the group. In this way, the group social system is kept intact. This dynamic is the reason our society has been so reluctant, and is just now starting to see and speak about the problem of abuse and bullying.

Parents may be unaware of the extent of the problem in the lives of their children because kids don't always talk and parents often do not ask. Dr. Olweus states that parents are often the last to know about this private shame in the lives of their children. The older the child, the less likely that child is to share this misery with parents.

Shame is attached to certain acts and attitudes. Among those postures is appearing to be a victim in any way. This is the same attitude that holds victims responsible in some way for being raped. I often hear people say that the victim must have done something to deserve it. Parents and other adults often find a reason citing appearance or personality or other characteristics that somehow make the target different from the rest of the peer group. Usually, these characteristics are things that cannot be changed. From a victim's perspective, these reasons are not a cause for hope or empowerment.

Victims come to feel ashamed and humiliated because they have been singled out to be a target for abuse. They come to know that the adults to whom they have turned for relief believe that they deserve the abuse or are unable to weigh the intent behind these experiences. Knowing that they cannot change the characteristics that make them so repulsive, targets stop trying to get help from the very adults who are supposed to protect them and teach them how to live.

When victims believe they bear shame, and no one can or will protect them from retaliation, they see no reason to tell or report incidents committed against them. The isolation of this situation, the shame and hopelessness are the seeds of the depression and despair which soon follows.

Tina stopped telling us what was happening. She did not want us to know how deeply she was hated. She was ashamed because she couldn't figure out how to turn the situation around. This shame and blame affect influences parents as well. As her mother, I struggled with the same kind of feelings and thought processes.

I had turned to the school for help. One of the teachers I had spoken with told me that she had seen how upset Tina had been in class but it was her policy not to intervene in "that teenage girl angst" because it "is all part of growing up and will take care of itself."

She said it would take too much time and that paying attention to it would give it power.

When parents try to advocate for their children, and the adults to whom they turn imply that the child has somehow asked for it or for some reason deserve it, parents often choose to "toughen up" themselves. Parents blame themselves for overreacting and somehow making it difficult for the child to get past it. These are common responses in bully situations.

I scoured my brain to try to figure out what it was that made our child so repulsive that she had become the target of contempt. I asked myself why she couldn't "just toughen up" or "ignore it?" I asked myself where we had fallen short in raising our child to be a victim. It took me a while to admit that I had little control over these things. They were the actions of a bully, and are not our fault.

In 2001, researcher Tonja Nansel, of the National Institute of Child Health and Human Development, reported that there is not enough being done to prevent this form of violence in our schools. She believes that instead of being treated as a tragedy, bullying is accepted as a normal rite of passage in American culture.

In her 2003 book, *The Bully, The Bullied and the Bystander*, Barbara Colorosa, reported another study conducted in 2001 by the *Kaiser Foundation*, *Nickelodeon TV* and *Children Now*, in which three-quarters of preteens interviewed reported that bullying is a regular occurrence at school and that it becomes even more pervasive as kids start high school. On the next page she said, "Research shows that parents and teachers greatly underestimate the frequency of bullying compared to student responses."

As parents, we are the only ones who will advocate for our children. As we learn more about this problem, we will come to understand that the shame and guilt belong to a society that turns the other way and blames the victim. We must understand that by definition there is nothing a child can do to deserve to be bullied. By definition, bullying is a top-down, one-way dynamic. We must speak out for change in our schools and in our society. We must empower ourselves to stand firm and to hold each other responsible to keep our children safe and to teach them how to respect and support each other. If we don't do it, who will? If we don't do it, what will happen to those we hold most dear? What will happen to our world?

We made the decision to get our daughter out of the abusive situation-the school system, instead of pursuing justice and healing within it. We did this after many failed attempts to remain in the system. We did this after our attempts, unsupported by the educational system, only seemed to produce an escalation of estrangement and abuse. After Tina's death we remained broken and troubled by the depth of power that bully-abuse has over children, the school, and the community, and the lack of understanding, knowledge, and interventions available. But we were determined to 'fix it'...ourselves...and the system.

Along with a few of Tina's old classmates and a handful of caring friends, we started a non-profit organization whose purpose was to develop programs that could be used in schools and organizations working with youth. *The Power of One Foundation* produced a video where Tina's friends talked openly about what happened to her and their own experiences with peer abuse. This video is being used by a number of school systems in their anti-bullying efforts. We also established pilot programs that were implemented in an area high school and middle school.

My husband and I have gone on to help develop and run the first private online high school in Minnesota; we prayed to find such a resource when Tina was still in the local high school.

Our daughter died around the same time as Jared High. Brenda searched the Internet, as we did, looking for support. We found each other and have been working together ever since. Since that time, caring parents, survivors, and Bully Police USA have been instrumental in getting anti-bullying laws passed in 43 states out of 48. A network of support has been developed and, at this writing, there are state volunteers of Bully Police USA in 48 states, and 9 countries besides the United States.

bullycide
IN AMERICA

MOMS SPEAK OUT
ABOUT THE
BULLYING/SUICIDE
CONNECTION

Compiled by Brenda High

On September 29, 1998, when her son Jared took his life, Brenda's life changed forever. As a result, Brenda testified to the Washington State House Education Committee on the subject of bullying, pushing for passage of an anti bullying law. It was signed into law in March 2002. Soon after, Brenda founded Bully Police USA, which reports on State Anti Bullying Laws and advocates for children who are bullied in school.

Brenda is the webmaster of
www.JaredStory.com
www.BullyPolice.org and
www.Bullycide.org

She has consulted with media, television and lawmakers as well as telling Jared's story to educators, students and parents. Brenda has appeared as a guest on "Judge Alex" and told her story on "E! Investigates: Bullying".

Brenda has spoken about Bullying, Depression, Suicide/Bullycide, healing from loss and numerous other subjects to many groups, organizations and conferences around the USA. To find out more about Brenda, a mom on a mission to stop school bullying, go to www.BrendaHigh.com.

Contributors

Elizabeth Bennett; http://www.peerabuse.info – Book: "Peer Abuse Know More" - Bullying from a Psychological Perspective taking the problem of bullying to a whole other dimension. Her book can be found on Amazon.

Glenn R. Stutzky, L.M.S.W., M.S.W. is a national expert on bullying serving on the faculty of Michigan State University's School of Social Work.

Catherine Hogan, Bully Police USA's National Consultant, is a licensed clinical social worker, certified school social worker, and clinical instructor/supervisor at the Yale Child Study Center.

Family, Career and Community Leaders of America – FCCLA
FCCLA's mission is to promote personal growth and leadership development through Family and Consumer Sciences Education. To learn more, call 703-476-4900 or visit FCCLA's website at www.fcclainc.org

Contributing Writers

Michelle Calco
Since that tragic day when Michelle experienced the loss of her eldest daughter, Kristina, on Dec. 4th, 2005, she has become actively involved in her local AFSP Out of the Darkness Community Walk, the Kalamazoo County Suicide Prevention Committee, BPUSA, and has written several viewpoint articles for her local paper, the Kalamazoo Gazette.

Tammy Epling - www.freewebs.com/mattepling
Since the tragic loss of her son Matt, Tammy and her husband Kevin have devoted their time to raising awareness of bullying and hazing in school. Being vocal on the issue has encouraged community forums and anti-bullying training in schools for parents, teachers and students alike.

Summer Himes
Summer's life is her family. She enjoys being a grandma and spending time with her children and grandchildren. Because of her bi-polar disorder and the trauma of losing April, Summer is disabled. She loves a good joke and laughter – it keeps the depression at bay.

Debra Johnston

Debra founded *Students For Safer Schools*, is a certified presenter for the *Bully Safe curriculum*, a *Bully Police Florida Co-Director* and has been a speaker at several statewide conferences, bringing Jeff's Story to students across the state in school assemblies. Debra worked with Governor Jeb Bush and Representative Ellyn Bogdanoff to create the Jeffrey Johnston "Stand Up For All Students" Act, which finally passed in 2008. Now Debra is working as the Bully Police USA Legislative Liaison to get a national anti bullying statute that will cover cyberbullying crimes.

Judith M. Kuczynski

Judy Kaczynski's daughter, Tina, was a victim of severe school harassment. After a bomb exploded in the family mailbox, Tina agreed to start over in a new school. A year later she died in a car accident. Judy is the President of Bully Police USA and is the co-founder and vice president of the Power of One Foundation, Inc., a non-profit organization studying relational aggression and bullying in schools.

Cathy Swartwood Mitchell

Cathy found her place in the anti bullying movement through telling Brandon's Story and bringing awareness. When Senator Rozell introduced the anti bullying bill to the Oklahoma Senate, Cathy introduced the Senate to the reality of bullying through Brandon's Story. The message was clear. On April 22, 2002, Oklahoma lawmakers passed the School Bullying Prevention Act. Cathy now serves as a Bully Police USA Board Member.

Adrianna Sgarlata Schweizer

At 9 years old, Adrianna felt the pain of bullying and it almost cost her life. It hurt her self confidence, taking years to regain it. "I don't want to ever forget those feelings, but I want to use them to help others", Adrianna says. Now, as the former Miss Virginia 2006, and the Virginia Director of Bully Police USA, Adrianna continues to speak out about bullying. She can be contacted by email at asgarlata@hotmail.com.

Rochelle Sides

Rochelle Sides is a wife, mother and grandmother. When Rochelle's daughter Corinne took her life on October 6th, 2004 after being bullied, Rochelle began her fight against bullies and the lack of education and programs that protect them. In 2005, Rochelle helped to pass the first anti bullying law was passed in The State of Texas.

Robin Todd

Robin is the Director of Bully Police Arizona, is Certified in Bullies & Victims Prevention Training and is a speaker and consultant. Robin's focus is on educating and raising awareness of, and prevention for, school bullying; the connection between bullying and other forms of violence, and the devastating effects bullying has on children. She is available to speak at schools, church groups and community programs – www.Bullycide.org/robin.html.

Chris & Eric Reading – The Readings

On The Readings' website, www.thereadings.net, branding, and imaging distinguishes them from the typical independent artists; they are on a mission, dedicating their lives to effecting change through music. Together, they write music to entertain, motivate and inspire.

Wanda's Song, perhaps their most artistic and poignant creation, has been circulated around the internet and picked up by several groups and individuals leading the charge against bullying in schools. The Readings are proud to be a part of a grass roots effort to end bullying, contributing to this book and protecting victims everywhere. Wanda's Song can be found at www.thereadings.net/wandas-song

About the Back Cover

The flag on the back cover was made by the children of Woodlawn Christian School in Prince George, VA. The children made a paper quilt after being told by Miss Virginia, **Adrianna Sgarlata (Schweizer)**, some of the stories of Bullycides. Their slogan - "*These little hands will Never hurt another Child*", *was printed among the hand prints of each child.*

Lyrics to Wanda's Song (If You Were Me)

Chris Reading, Eric Reading, John Paul Lourence

Wanda was the one girl we claimed we never knew
Lincoln High School's homely-coming queen
She barely graduated with the class of '92
Voted most unlikely to succeed

Rumor had it Wanda never knew who her daddy was
At least that's what we spread all over town
I guess we always thought that we were building ourselves up
With the sticks and stones we threw to break her down

All the years we thought it didn't matter
Cuz we never saw her cry
And Wanda never asked us

Chorus
Why, do you hurt me, and treat me like you do
What have I ever done to, deserve this, from you
Would you do the things you do
If you were me and I were you

Looking back I see the pain that we put Wanda thru
And just where all the fun and games were leading
We didn't realize the damage sticks and stones would do
Cuz it was deep inside Wanda was bleeding

The paper said her death was self-inflicted
But was it suicide?
Cuz the note she wrote said...

Repeat Chorus

Bridge
For every action there's reaction
Broken hearts don't just happen
If you put yourself in their position
There's no good answer to the question ...

Repeat Chorus
Tag: Wanda was the one girl we claimed we never knew

Made in United States
Orlando, FL
10 May 2022

17718238R00085